I0149876

ABSENT IN PRESENCE
BUT NOT IN HEART

A Christian Educator's Guide
to Online Learning

ISBN #: 1-931178-74-7

©2004 Joshua Reichard, Vision Publishing. All rights reserved.
Ramona, CA 92065

www.vision.edu

Absent in Presence but not in Heart

ABSENT IN PRESENCE BUT NOT IN HEART

A Christian Educator's Guide to Online Learning

Joshua David Reichard, M.A.

Absent in Presence but not in Heart

Dedication:

"This text is dedicated to my lovely wife, Sara,
who encouraged me through months of research writing
as I completed my master's thesis from which this text was derived.
Without her insight, encouragement, and consistent prayer,
what you are about to read would not exist.
May we have a long life of fruitful ministry together.
I love you, Sara."

In Memory of:

Andrew Brandt Eddy
"Committed Christian and Computer Scientist"
1972 – 2001

Absent in Presence but not in Heart

Acknowledgements:

I would like to acknowledge the following individuals who have contributed to my spiritual, professional, and academic development over the years:

1. To Pastors Dave and Kathie Thomas for believing in God's call on Sara and I and supporting us in our mission to El Salvador.

2. To Reverend Frank Hodges, for demonstrating to me the true meaning of vocational ministry and the character of a theologian and a man of God.

3. To Dr. Stan DeKoven and Dr. Steve Deckard for being academic role models and rigorously critiquing this text.

4. To Mrs. Nancy Collier and Dr. Benna Ewig for demonstrating to me the heart of an educator at a very young age.

5. To Shawn Blake for first introducing me to the art and science of computer programming.

6. To David Richardson, for teaching me more about computers than all of the technical manuals I have ever read.

7. To Marty Johnson, for being the first to believe in my call to a combination of technology and ministry.

8. To my mother and father for believing in my ambition enough to make that first sacrificial purchase of a home computer many years ago.

Absent in Presence but not in Heart

Table of Contents

Absent in Presence but not in Heart

Introduction:
The Worldwide Advancement

Figuratively, let's consider the Bible to be the first "website". From the comprehensive Histories of the Pentateuch to the voluminous doctrines of Paul in the Epistles, the pages of scripture were documents composed for specific audiences, but of vital interest and intended accessibility to the entire human race... each uniquely woven together. Much like an Internet website, God's Divine Word to humanity was intended for worldwide accessibility.

Throughout the ages, the written Word of God has ravaged the barriers of language and culture. It has crossed the boundaries of mountains and seas. It has survived the clouded generations of men, withstanding the rising and falling of empires, the coming and going of kings. As the first formally printed text and retaining its position as the world's best-seller, the Bible is the only "eternal media".

The Internet has become a communication vehicle of comparable proportions. Within seconds, the simplest of men can publish their personal treatise to a worldwide audience. The same phenomenon that the Biblical documents have gravely endured over centuries can be bypassed by a twenty-first century dreamer with the effortless click of a button.

Sacred texts and teachings no longer need to be secured in caves along the shores of the Dead Sea. They no longer need to be etched in stone or tightly packed into a dusty sarcophagus. For a few dollars a month, one's magnum opus can be digitally cosseted in an underground bunker of networked servers, clad with iron and doubly shielded by armed guards.

Modern texts hardly need to be petrified or isolated in burial tombs; they can be made thoroughly accessible and potentially available for the entire world to browse at leisure. This is the era of the World Wide Web.

During the apostolic age, the need for a worldwide communication system was desperate. The Early Church had only the network of roads and sea passages implemented by the Roman Empire to carry the Gospel to the ends of the earth. In this present age, the byways of horses and ships have been antiquated by fiber-optic and satellite networks.

Educational Ministry and Distance Learning: Facing the reality of technological advancement

The Apostle Paul was a distance educator[1]. Although he frequented his pupils with missionary visits, his canonized letters were delivered through a period-relative distance learning system. So to speak, the Body of Christ still derives its doctrine by browsing Paul's "web pages".

The apostolic model of writing epistles to targeted, local bodies of believers was decidedly "distance" in nature. Modern day missionaries who are responsible for braving new territories and planting new churches, must accept the fact that the Internet is presently the most cost-effective, wide-reaching tool available for discipleship and training where possible. In the first century, letters via hand delivery were the best method available for Paul to reach his

---

[1] See "Baker's Guide to Christian Distance Education", Baker, Jason D. Website: http://www.bakersguide.com

students. That era is long past. Today, those who have a burden for educational ministry should be pining for rich multimedia and interactive systems to deliver their curriculum, not parchment and ink. The world is changing... the church is changing... the way in which we must approach the Great Commission is indeed changing.

Distance Education for preparing men and women for vocational ministry is not a new concept for the modern church. Theological Education by Extension (TEE), first formally introduced by the Presbyterian Church in Guatemala[2], has been adopted (in some form or another) by every major Protestant denomination as well as the Roman Catholic Church. This method of training has successfully equipped countless vocational ministers and lay people during the last century who would have not been able to reach a traditional seminary.

However, never before has the Church been presented with such an amazing opportunity to now reach the world with theological education and ministerial training. To most Christians, the advent of the Internet and its potential to reach the world is not a fresh revelation. Present technology has been heralded by some Christians as the ultimate platform for evangelism and hated by many because of its perversion by the Enemy. But nevertheless, the undeniable fact is that it provides the platform for an advancement of biblical truth in ways never before dreamed of. The Bible itself is a stalwart example of this phenomenon... over thousands of years it has cross the boundaries of space, time, language and culture. Today, the Internet provides an accelerated opportunity for this same process to take place for every ounce of biblical truth and curriculum the Church can muster. Of course, the Word of God itself is at the very forefront of this rapid advancement.

Microsoft Corporation founder and chairman, Bill Gates, stated, "A revolution is upon us. Revolutions are a way of life in the computer industry. Only 20 years ago, the world was still in the

---

[2] See PCUSA's website, "Global Education and International Leadership Development" at http://www.pcusa.org/globaled/kinsler.htm

mainframe era. Few people had access to or used computers, and when they did, it was only through the nearest Information Technology department. The Personal Computer, the graphical user interface, and the introduction of the Internet changed all that. They democratized computing for hundreds of millions of people and transformed the computer into a mass-market product"[3].

Now more than ever before, the Word of God can be placed into the hands of the masses. Post-secondary Christian Educators in today's colleges and seminaries or missionaries laboring in the field, must recognize that online training and delivery of curriculum is an inevitable step toward the biblical mandate of Christ Himself to "disciple all nations (Matthew 28:19)"[4].

Maintaining spiritual activation and accountability in the new "digital wineskin"

Christian Educators are now faced with the challenge of utilizing the Internet as the modern method for distance education. Perhaps the old wineskins for educational delivery systems are gently wearing thin and eagerly awaiting a new wineskin that will accommodate the needs of a world that is desperate for rich discipleship and training. Perhaps this new wineskin is a digital one.

If so, there are many spiritual issues that must be forthrightly addressed in preparation for the transition. When the wine is transferred from one wineskin to another, not one drop of good wine should be lost (Matthew 9:17)[5]. The challenge for Christian educators in the years to come will be maintaining every ounce of the good wine of theological education and spiritual

---

[3] This quote was taken from Page 5 of the 2002 Microsoft Developer's Network (MSDN) announcement of the release of the .NET technology (print).
[4] The Great Commission should always be understood as the process of discipling nations, not merely converting them. This strategic development of the Body of Christ is accomplished through the cooperation of the five-fold ministry gifts of Ephesians 4:11 via training, education, and practical ministry experience.
[5] While it is clearly understood that within the context of this passage, Jesus was speaking of the old and new covenants, this principle can be applied as an analogy to nearly any transition from tradition to new ideas or methods.

empowerment in the transition from traditional textbooks, chalkboards, lecture halls and classrooms to the Internet and interactive technology.

When my wife and I were training in our pre-field orientation as Assemblies of God missionary associates, I heard a striking phrase I will never forget, lightheartedly delivered by the regional director of Africa: "If you ever want to legitimize anything you do, in ministry or otherwise, simply call it a paradigm shift."

Of course, this dear brother in Christ was only being cynical as he said this very tongue-in-cheek. However, there was much wisdom in what he said, as the buzzword "paradigm-shift" can be used rather haphazardly to try to legitimize change. I assure you, this technological shift in education is far more than a "paradigm shift"; it is a reality that is already in full-swing in both secular and sacred education. In this very strategic hour of history, the Church does not need shifted paradigms... it needs to make a strategic decision on how it will utilize the tools of this present age for the furtherance of the Kingdom of God and the fulfillment of the Great Commission.

Absent in Presence but not in Heart

Chapter One:
Foundations of Online Learning

Before we begin to thoroughly examine the problems and effects of the educational convergence of theology and technology, there are some terms and concepts which will be used throughout the remainder of this book, which I wish to clarify:

- Online and Internet, will be used as corresponding terms. I understand there is a distinction between the two terms, but they are often used interchangeably.

- Educator and Instructor, will also be used as corresponding terms. Many of principles that will be presented will be applicable to both the vocational educator and an "instructor" of an individual course or topic.

- Activation, for purposes of this book, will be defined as the life changing experience of spiritual formation which empowers the student for effective ministry. While secular education requires only a cognitive accumulation and comprehension of knowledge and skills, ministerial and theological academics must convict and empower the student to grow in deeper intimacy with Jesus Christ and in greater submission to the work of the Holy Spirit in the world and in their personal lives. When spiritual maturity fails to perpetuate in the life of the student, activation for ministry (therefore, competency for the vocation of ministry) also fails to occur. The Apostle Paul longed for his pupils to become more Christ like (Galatians 4:19) and thus more mature by evidencing particular qualities in their everyday life. This appropriation of truth and change of character is the only manifestation of true activation for the ministry[6]. It is also the only fruit of Christian Education which is entirely pleasing to God (Romans 14:18, 2 Corinthians 5:9, Galatians 1:10, Ephesians 5:10, Colossians 1:10, 1 Thessalonians 4:1) and the only fruit which will bring Him glory as the student is commissioned to fulfill his or her life calling (Romans 15:6, 2 Corinthians 4:15, Ephesians 1:12,14, 2 Thessalonians 1:12). Distinct from all technical skills, talent, and ambition, a lack of activation, that is spiritual formation and empowerment, indicates that the student has not been adequately trained to serve in a Divine calling.

- Accountability, for purposes of this book, will be defined as consistent, truthful, transparent communication and interaction between two or more people wherein spiritual growth is assessed, challenged, and matured. Proverbs 21:17 states, "As iron sharpens iron, so one man sharpens another." A student training for ministry must be held accountable daily by a personal mentor or mentors and peers within his or her own church or community. A student who studies alone online without being in covenant relationship with a nearby human being is in far greater danger of a spiritual failure or stagnation than one who is held perpetually accountable by an entire student caucus, administration, and professors in a traditional learning environment. This principle is clearly indicated in scripture: "two are better than one, because they have a good return for their work: If one falls down, his friend can help him up. But pity the man who falls and has no one to help him up! Also, if two lie down together, they will keep warm. But how can one keep warm alone? Though one may be overpowered, two can defend

---

[6] Zuck, *Teaching as Paul Taught.* Page 117.

themselves. A cord of three strands is not quickly broken (Ecclesiastes 4:9-12)."

Scope and Limitations:

I will make this point very clear: what we will be exploring is admittedly limited by present technology. Be it understood that technology is rapidly improving and expanding and the conclusions drawn regarding the deficiencies of technology are entirely limited to the present technologies available for Internet-based instruction. I do believe, however, that the theological principles presented will permeate any advance in technology that the future has to offer.

I will not take into account specific technological applications, software, hardware, services, or devices; rather it will address the issues surrounding Internet technologies as a whole by means of a more theoretical approach. Overly technical terminology and precise development strategies will be intentionally avoided. I offer my sincerest apologies to any fellow software engineers, but this is primarily a theological text and secondarily a technical one.

It is also worth clarifying one more point, although I trust that I have made it relatively clear. This study shall also be limited to theological education; because spiritual issues shall be directly addressed, the study does not necessarily apply to secular vocations. For instance, the same learning theories for teaching apologetics will not apply to teaching agriculture.

A basic hypothesis and problem statement:
How to approach online educational ministry

In an effort to make the principles in this book coherent and purposeful, it would be appropriate to establish a formal hypothesis by which I can continually orient my investigations and you can relate each topic. A simple hypothesis which summarizes my goals for this book follows:

"*Internet-based distance education is an essential component for modern theological and ministerial training; however, it fails to inherently provide students with adequate Spiritual Activation and Accountability.*"

In like manner, the foundational question which I will continually attempt to answer is:

"*Is it possible for Christian Educators to address the issues of Activation and Accountability so that Internet technology may be utilized to the fullest without sacrificing these critical, spiritual components of the learning process?*"

Using these two statements, we have a very good map and compass by which this book can be navigated. As you read, continue to lean back on the hypothesis and to the foundational question as the Holy Spirit speaks to your own heart.

A purpose for understanding online learning:

While we have a developed hypothesis and foundational question to base our investigations on, it would also be appropriate to develop a purpose statement. It reads as follows:

"*This book will demonstrate the present need for the utilization of technology in theological and ministerial education and training while addressing the problems surrounding these two essential elements of spiritual formation, proving that the former cannot be entirely successful unless the latter is addressed. In simpler terms, this text will equip Christian Educators to utilize online learning and Internet technologies more effectively.*"

Rationale:

Internet-based theological and ministerial education is only in its developmental infancy, but as technology continues to evolve, more effective means of communication are continually adding to its legitimacy and usability for purposes of the advancement of the Kingdom of God and the discipling of the nations. The essential elements of Activation and Accountability may never be directly addressed by virtual systems, but strategic alternatives exist which work in conjunction with Internet-based learning to compensate.

Notwithstanding, the Internet and the potential it yields for worldwide discipleship and training must be embraced as one of the most effective means of educational ministry the Body of Christ has ever seen. By embracing new technology and maximizing its effectiveness for the advancement of the Kingdom (all the while effectively addressing its spiritual inadequacies), the modern Church may experience the greatest harvest in the history of humanity.

I believe, with all my heart that the Church is at this pivotal point in history. Systems for communication have evolved more in the past century than the collective ages of the earth's history. Never before have we seen communication systems advance so rapidly... and they continue to develop more with each passing day. In my short lifetime, I have seen incredible technological advancements. I can only imagine what my children and grandchildren will see. The rationale for taking hold of the wonderful methods available to today's Christian Educators is simply this: to establish a base, no matter how primitive, for future generations to successfully build upon if the Lord should tarry. If we strive to understand and utilize online learning to the best of our ability today, we can rest assured that tomorrow's missionary endeavors will be all the more successful. Ever so, let it be Lord Jesus. Amen.

Significance:

If Internet-based theological and ministerial education can be properly implemented, it will equip a fresh generation of ministers and theologians to do the work of the ministry unlike those who have gone before them. Leaders trained online may bring astounding transformation to the way in which the Church approaches people, nations, ministry, and education. Indeed, today's ministers stand at a very distinct crossroads in history where the sacred halls of the seminary may soon be replaced by virtual terminals of modern technology. This is an issue that Christians must address today, in this hour. The need is urgent.

Failing to do so may produce a generation of clergy who are incompetent, unsanctified, and self-instructed. My desire, as is yours, I pray, is to develop a generation of ministers who are efficient, effective, and empowered for a productive life of ministry. The ultimate outcome of the online learning phenomenon will depend on the way in which today's Christian Educators decide to approach this emerging method of theological and ministerial education. If you are reading this text, then I trust that you are a Christian Educator. In that case, I then challenge you to take hold of this vision for tomorrow's generation and let the Lord use your gifts and talents for the great labor which awaits us in the world which is white unto harvest. You are part of this great plan to reach and teach the nations of the world.

Chapter Two:
Christians and Technology

It is said by some that the 20th Century birthed more technological and industrial advancement than all other centuries combined. Pause for a moment and contemplate that today's primary school students have never known a world with the Internet.

The Internet is the fastest growing communications media the world has ever seen. Radio existed for 38 years before it had 50 million listeners. Television took 13 years to get 50 million viewers. The Internet reached 50 million users in the United States in just 4 years[7]. The rapidly expanding technology of the Internet is being used extensively all over the world, not only for business or government, but by Christians as well. The Internet is not a secular phenomenon.

"The head and not the tail"

The uses of the Internet and its technologies are vast, but its function can be organized into two dominant categories -- Information and Communication. The most common use for Internet is certainly for "information discovery". There were periods of history past where information was controlled by the papal and political powers of the world--- and guarded from the masses. Today, an overwhelming amount of information is available to "anyone with a phone line and a

---

[7] Bridis, Ted. "Cyberspace is driving America's Economy," Pittsburgh Post Gazette, Vol 71, no. 259, 4/16/98. Page A-1.

personal computer"[8]. Like never before, a person can be connected to the limitless bytes of data the world has to offer. I remember when I was in elementary school, the closest thing we had to the Internet was a "Compton's Encyclopedia CD-ROM", which was a precious commodity since only one computer in the entire school had a CD-ROM drive... and it was one of the first. Though this may frighten many of today's students, most of my reports in elementary and Junior High were done with old-fashioned encyclopedias and books from the library. If you are a Christian Educator over the age of 25, then you can most certainly appreciate this point as well. It seems, however, that the rigorous requirements of diligent study and research has, in one way or another, diminished or evolved into a point and click procedure.

George Barna has even gone as far as to name a new generation of young people (born 1985-2002) the "Mosaic Generation". In a Pastors.com interview, Barna states, "We gave them the name Mosaics because - as we were examining who they are, how they think, and how they live - the one thing that kept coming back to us is the thought, Wow, they're a little bit of everything. They're mosaic in every aspect of their life."[9] One of the issues attributing to this factor is that these young people have instant access to any information their curiosity could possibly invoke. They simply sign-on to the Internet and find a "snippet" or a "clip" of information or media and to satisfy their need for knowledge. This makes them "mosaic", so to speak; their ability to pick and choose information applicable to virtually any aspect of life almost as freely as choosing a meal from the menu of a fast-food restaurant. Imagine for a moment that these young people will be the missionaries, pastors, evangelists, and prophetic voices of tomorrow.

---

[8] Demy, Timothy J. "Technology and Theology: Reality an Hope for the Third Millennium", in Issues 2000: Evangelical Faith and Cultural Trends in the New Millennium, edited by Mal Couch (Grand Rapids: Kregal, 1999). Page 47.

[9] From Richard Land's interview with George Barna on Pastors.com, 2003. For more information see Barna's book, "Real Teens: A Contemporary Snapshot of Youth Culture".

The Internet trend is not isolated to the "new generation". In 2001, 149 Million Americans used the Internet. George Barna reported that the most widespread use of the Internet among Americans is finding information[10].

History has proven that religious groups are typically resistant to technological innovations, but Christians in the United States are now just as likely as the general American population to utilize new technology.

A study at the Barna Research Group revealed that "Born-again Christians have the same rate of adoption of modern technology as do those who are not born-again[11]. The technologies that Barna surveyed included VCRs, cable television, satellite television, DVDs, cellular telephones, desktop & laptop computers, handheld computers, CD-ROMs, and home Internet Access. Not only did the study disclose that Christians are embracing new technology, but it extends to the realm of personal ownership and usage. According to Barna, "two thirds of professing born-again Christians own a personal computer; of that number, fifty-six percent own a desktop computer, sixteen percent own a notebook/laptop computer, and seven percent own a handheld computer".

These figures are almost identical to the use of technology by the American population as a whole at fifty-five, sixteen, and eight percent respectively. Surprisingly, Christians are leading the overall population in desktop computer ownership by a snug margin of one. This, I believe, demonstrates that the majority of Christians, both laity and clergy, who are in need of discipleship and formal education alike, are at the helm of the technological revolution. The great task for the Church must now be to mobilize its educators in the same direction and with the same force as the populace.

---

[10] Barna Research Group, "More Americans are seeking Net-based Faith Experiences"; May 21, 2001. Internet Resource located at http://www.barna.org.
[11] Barna Research Group (2), "More Christians Embrace Technology"; June 12, 2000. Internet Resource located at http://www.barna.org.

Christians and Computer Ownership in the United States (2001)

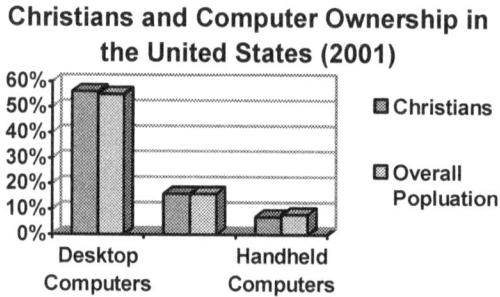

Figure 1.1 – Data according to The Barna Research Group.

Another staggering statistic from Barna reveals that "more than nine out of ten Senior Pastors use a computer at home or at the church. According to this research, it appears that Pastors are at the helm of the technological revolution; apart from sheer modesty, it would be difficult to find a Pastor in the United States who can truly take personal ownership of the designation "computer illiterate".

A *Christianity Today* survey revealed, however, that small churches, or churches with an annual budget under $100,000, struggle to keep up with computing trends. Only 73 percent of those churches own even one computer, while churches with larger budgets own at least two computers. Churches with an annual budget greater than $500,000 will, on average, own up to 5 computers[12]. Understandably, finances are always a consideration for any physical asset the church may require for operation. The study reveals a proportionate figure for computer ownership to church size and fiscal capability.

Born Again Evangelical Christians are every bit as likely to use the Internet as non-Christians. Barna's research reveals that forty-eight percent of adult Christians have some Internet access, compared to fifty percent of the entire population.

---

[12] LaRue, John C. Jr., "Special Report: Churches and Computers". July/August 1999. Christianity Today. Christianity Today International.

American Pastors are relying heavily on the Internet to modernize and their daily ministry. According to Barna, four-fifths (80%) of all Protestant Senior Pastors have access to the Internet, fifty percent of whom access the Internet on a daily basis. Barna also revealed that Pastors are more likely to maintain friendships, buy products, and have religious experiences on the Internet than those in other professions.

With Senior Pastors blazing a trail for their congregations, it is no surprise that one out of every three Protestant churches in the United States have an Internet website. Among the two-thirds of churches that do not have a presence on the web, nineteen percent say that they plan to do so within the next twelve months. There are many tools available to churches for quickly establishing a web presence, including a company called "E-zekiel"[13], which has "ready-made" web solutions for churches such as calendars, stores, and easy to use content management. Tools such as these are making presence on the web more and more of a viable option for today's churches.

According to the Pew Internet and American Life Project http://www.pewinternet.org), twenty-five percent of Internet users have searched the web for religious or spiritual information. More than three million people gather religious or spiritual information from the Internet every day. The Pew study also showed that more people have received religious or spiritual information online than have gambled, auctioned, traded stocks, placed phone calls, or used banking and dating services online[14]. This fact is, of course, quite significant for online Christian Educators.

The Pew study refers to Internet users who search for religious or spiritual information online (approximately twenty-five percent of all Internet users) as "Religious Surfers". The study proclaims that these users "treat the Internet as a vast ecclesiastical library and they hunt for general spiritual information online."

---

13 http://www.e-zekiel.com
[14] Pew Internet & American Life Project, "CyberFaith: How Americans Pursue Religion Online", December 23, 2001; Internet Resource located at http://www.pewinternet.org.

According to the Pew Study, the top five activities of "Religious Surfers" are:

1. Looking for information about their own faith (67%)
2. Looking for information about other faiths (50%)
3. Emailing a prayer request (38%)
4. Downloading religious music (38%)
5. Giving spiritual guidance via email (37%)

The study also revealed that in their most recent Internet usage session, "Religious Surfers" used the Internet to perform the following functions:

1. Find educational or devotional materials (40%)
2. Find general information about a religious faith (29%)
3. Communicated with people in their church (11%)

Barna also discovered that "the most attractive option to Christians was listening to religious teaching online". It is more than evident that the Body of Christ is searching for educational material online. This should be a resounding call to arms for Christian Educators everywhere to utilize the Internet to its fullest.

A survey conducted by *Christianity Today*[15], yielded similar results. It found that pastors are regularly using e-mail to stay in contact with people. The study revealed that 80% of today's pastors are e-mailing other pastors, 62% are e-mailing congregation members, 65% are e-mailing missionaries, 53% are e-mailing church leaders, and 38% are e-mailing visitors[16].

---

[15] In the Christianity Today study, one thousand surveys were mailed to [pastoral] subscribers of *Christianity Today* and *Leadership Journal* (500 each), and 564 were returned, for a response rate of 56 percent. Of respondents, 462 were pastors. The margin of error is plus or minus 5 percentage points.

[16] LaRue, John C. Jr., "The Internet: A blessing or curse for pastors?". March/April 2001. Christianity Today. Christianity Today International.

The study also discovered that pastors are using the Internet to help prepare their sermons and Bible studies, revealing that six of ten pastors online (61%) use Web sites to search for sermon illustrations and use Internet Bible and reference tools (another mode of educational delivery). About one-third (31%) have witnessed or shared the gospel online, usually with someone they already knew in person. Three percent of pastors have led someone to faith over the Internet.

The entire world is not yet as computer savvy as America or its industrialized sister nations. A pastor serving a congregation in Japan posted a comment to a TheOoze.com community article stating, "I serve a congregation that is about 95% online, in a nation that has cell phone saturation over 85%. I come from a country that is 65% online and has a cell phone saturation of about 35%. I am convinced that we will never be able to maximize our potential with technology in the Church [Body of Christ] until we have the kind of saturation that I am seeing in the International Church in Japan."[17]

As a whole, the Church (particularly the Church in America) is using computers and the Internet. This is neither a secular phenomenon nor a passing fad. What is happening within the Body of Christ concerning Internet communication is, I believe, a strategic moment in the destiny and history of the Church. Such technology must not be extinguished or ignored.

Jesus admonished his disciples:

> *"Ye are the light of the world. A city that is set on a hill cannot be hid. Neither do men light a candle, and put it under a bushel, but on a candlestick; and it giveth light unto all that are in the house. Let your light so shine before men, that they may see your good works, and glorify your Father which is in heaven." (Matthew 5:14-18)*

---

[17] Stanton-Rich, Michael. "What will it take? Some questions about technology and the Church". Internet Resource. http://www.theooze.com/articles.

As a lit candle would give light to a whole room, so it is the responsibility of this generation to perpetuate the mission of God to bring the gospel to the ends of the earth through the means made available to us; undoubtedly, the Internet and its worldwide communication networks is the chief of these. Any attempt of the church (educators in particular) to hinder the proclamation of the hope of Christ under a bushel by ignoring the power and possibilities that Internet presents would do nothing more than hinder the advancement of the gospel and the building of the Kingdom of God. The Body of Christ is being equipped with the technology they need to "connect". Now it is the responsibility of Christian Educators to provide them with the training they need to multiply and advance the Kingdom like never before.

Footnotes on the statistics presented in this chapter:

a. While the statistics in this chapter may quickly become outdated, I believe that they do demonstrate a powerful trend at a single moment in the history of the Church, which can be of great use to future generations.

b. A significant portion of the data and statistics from the various independent sources that have been presented in this chapter are explored in detail in the following research article compiled by Dr. Michael Vlach at TheologicalStudies.org, who has produced an excellent analysis of the impact of technology on the modern-day Church. I strongly recommend his website and the following article:

- *"How people of faith are using the Internet"*, by Michael J. Vlach. URL: http://www.pastors.com/article.asp?ArtID=2071 or http://www.theologicalstudies.org/internet.html

For more information on the impact of technology and the Internet on the Church, also refer to The Internet Church, by Walter P. Wilson.

Chapter Three:
Christians and the emerging online education market

There is something very new happening in the world. The online learning phenomenon is taking hold in every imaginable discipline. A businessman can earn his MBA online, a Registered Nurse can earn her BSN, and a minister can earn his or her Doctor of Ministry... virtually. Indeed, the realm of education is rapidly transforming and Christians are planted firmly in the dead center.

It is clear to see that the secular world is embracing online learning in ways most traditional educators never imagined. However, it is absolutely vital for Christians to draw a clear line of distinction between theological and ministerial training and every other profession that comfortably wedges itself into the online learning market. Christian Education has a dramatic role in this emerging market, but how well it will be implemented is yet to be determined.

Eschaton Magazine journalist Jack Van Deventer notes that, "the education market in the United States is approximately $1 trillion or 10% of the GNP. The market is expected to expand very quickly. Online delivery is one factor fueling rapid growth. Christians have been slow to offer educational services over the web, but look for that to change in the next few years." He continued by stating that Christians will soon "find themselves in the driver's seat" as Christian Education rises to successful implementation and government education deteriorates[18].

Richard Bishirijan, the founder of Yorktown University, a secular distance learning college on the Internet, stated that "government-funded schools have an incentive to produce government-loving citizens. Yorktown's marketing plan aims to attract a student body of primarily, conservatives, evangelical Christians, prepared home school students, members of the military, free-market thinkers, and others. We want to engender a generation who is well-educated and well grounded..."

A 2001 study conducted by Merill Lynch analysts revealed that the online education market was serving nearly 2.2 million students by the end of that year; this number continues to grow with each passing year of the 21st Century. Jones International University was the first private, Internet-based education institution to receive regional accreditation, and shortly after its success, many Christian colleges and universities emerged to follow its lead. In turn, Christian Education continues to rise to the top of this powerfully emerging market, both in the United States and abroad.[19]

It is clear that Christians are being viewed in a new light, not as the religious cynics who take centuries to adopt new technology, but as the forerunners in a great advance toward a global system of online distance education and training.

We must take heed at this critical moment in history... to maintain integrity in our implementation of online systems of Christian Education; spiritual integrity in the eyes of God first and foremost, and academic integrity in the eyes of traditionalists. With a proper understanding of the online learning environment and a well-developed theology to properly form it, this goal is not out of reach for today's Christian Educators.

---

[18] Van Deventer, Jack. "The Academic Transition". *Eschaton Magazine*. December, 2000.

[19] See Talcott, Alexander. "Education Online?". The Dartmouth Review.

A missiological perspective:
How the nations of the world are using
technology and the Internet

As a Christian Educator with firsthand experience on the mission field and heart for the nations, I feel as though an exploration of the online learning in the Two-Thirds World is necessary to develop a proper perspective of how the global Church may perceive this method of instruction. If we are to explore the Church's role in this phenomenon, then let us take into account a broader picture of what the international Church is facing.

The number of Internet users worldwide will expand from 300 million [in 2000] to one billion by 2005 (as many as 150 million new users were poised to connect to the Internet in that year), according to a $1 million study spanning 34 countries carried out by the Angus Reid Group[20], which operates out of Toronto. The study found that United States and Canadian citizens lead the world in Internet usage. Sweden, the Netherlands, Finland, and Australia approach the U.S. and Canada in terms of being Internet-savvy. This comes as no surprise as these two nations are often the first of which come to mind when the designation of "Westernized Nations" is invoked. European and Japanese users were found to be the most likely to use Web-enabled wireless devices. Per-minute phone charges are also a factor which is driving the use of wireless web devices in Europe and Asia.

In 1998, China already had more than one million Internet users, Japan had crossed the 10 million user mark, and there were more than 500,000 estimated Internet users in India.[21]

However, worldwide growth patterns of Internet usage suggest that only a few countries will experience a real boom in

---

[20] Rao, Madanmohan, "Governance of the Internet", CPSR Newsletter, Fall, 1998, 16(4).
[21] Stone, Martin. "Study Shows 300 Mil Worldwide Web Users" Newsbytes, excerpted in: ACM TechNews, Volume 2, Issue 34: Friday, March 24, 2000.

Internet use. The study also revealed that ownership of home computers and interest in the Internet is lowest among Eastern and Southern Europeans; perhaps because of the years of war and poverty which has delivered an inhibiting blow to this region.

The study also stated that, "Wireless Web access on cell phones and palmtops and public access to the Web in cafes and kiosks must play a greater role in bridging the digital divide". I have found this to be true in Latin America. "Ciber Cafés" as they are called, can be found on almost every corner of the major cities. The thought of an average income family in this region owning a computer with an Internet connection is yet unthinkable, but it is not beyond imagination for a large percentage of twenty-somethings to have an e-mail address or Instant Messenger screen name, which they access at their local kiosk or ciber café. Such services are indeed bridging the digital divide, making technology, especially the connectively of the Internet, accessible to the masses.

At the time of the study, about 59 percent of Americans had Internet access, followed by 56 percent of Canadians, and 53 percent of Swedes. A greater percentage of Northern Europeans than Southern Europeans were found to use the Internet. Germany had 18 million Internet users, positioning them for third place in Europe-- followed by 14 million in the United Kingdom.

Communication infrastructure is a major inhibiting factor for the Two-Thirds World. A clear example of this can be seen in the effort of the United States to rebuild Iraq... wherein discussions are taking place to establish the nation's first cellular phone network.

The ten richest countries (which contain 20% of the world population) have three quarters of all telephone mainlines. The average density of telephone mainlines in developing countries is 5.2 per 100 persons while in industrialized countries it is 52.3. There is an immense difference in telephone availability in Third World regions, where most telephone lines are in urban areas. In rural Africa with 78% of the population [of third world regions] there are only 228,000 lines in total. This means that 1,700 people should technically share one telephone.

Telephone density in Third World Regions

Region	Number of telephone lines per 100 persons
Central and East Europe	18
Latin America	8
Asia	5
Africa	1.6

Of Africa's 700 Million inhabitants only 0.1% of the population presently has access to the Internet. 550,000 of its Internet users come from the Republic of South Africa, 50,000 come from North Africa and only 40,000 come from the other countries[22]. The University of South Africa (UNISA) has long been a pioneering world leader in the Distance Education market. It is presently implementing its own virtual online learning environment for its wide variety of academic programs, which may prove to attract more western students than those who speak Afrikaans.

While these regions with poor communications infrastructure were once listed among the "forgotten nations" of Christendom, they are now experiencing an explosion of evangelical expansion. Many have been historically regarded as "Third World Countries" are now being identified as "Emerging-Growth Countries" where Education, Telecommunications, and Computer Technology are rising to the top of their respective local economies.

Recent studies also reveal that the global epicenter of Christianity is shifting southward from the once prominent

---

[22] Servatie, Alain et all: "European Community Cooperation with Countries in Transitation and Developing Countries in Telecommunications and Information Society", in Health, Information Society and Developing Countries, Editor Marcelo C. Sosa-Tudicissa et all, IOS Press 1995. Online Resource found at http://www.uni-muenster.de/EthnologieHeute/eh1/afe.htm.

leadership of Europe and the United States, to the regions of Latin America, Northern Africa, and the South Pacific, including China and Indonesia; many of which are comprised of the Third World nations. These Third World missionaries, like unto the "Eleventh-Hour Laborers" of Matthew 20, will undoubtedly become the missionary force of the 21st century. The Western world, rich in resources, must do everything possible to empower Third World missions with the technological tools they will need to accomplish what will perhaps be the greatest harvest the Global Church has ever know[23].

The Nations and
Internet-based theological and ministerial training

Dr. Gary Wolfram, a professor of political economy at Hillsdale College and one of the founding faculty members of the entirely Internet-based Yorktown University, believes that while an online education will never replace what educators can offer in the classroom, "e-schools" have advantages over the traditional educational experience. Costs are minimized by eliminating the "facility component" and there is an exciting ability to unite students across the globe who share comparable ideologies (i.e. Christians). Wolfram acknowledges, "I can convey more information in my classroom than I can over the Internet," but adds "If you're in Guatemala, you can't come to my classroom"[24].

One of the most important contributions that Internet-based distance education makes is its ability to provide access to education to those who would otherwise be denied it. While technological limitations may continue to hinder widespread availability, the power of the Internet as the delivery system of choice has been widely acclaimed in Third World regions. Richard Dodds suggests that many of the Third World regions focus on providing primary and secondary educational opportunities to the entire population before

---

[23] See Jenkins, Philip: "The Next Christendom: The Coming of Global Christianity"
[24] Talcott, Alexander. "Education Online?". The Dartmouth Review.

government-supported colleges and universities are considered[25]. In a day when the demand for higher education continues to increase, but the resources to address the demand remain limited, the gap between those who have access to post-secondary education and those who do not continues to widen[26].

Many of the Third World nations have, however, been open to supporting extension services such as Internet-based education, wherein distance learning has been seen as one possible way of expanding educational opportunities rapidly.

With the surge of technological acceptance among Christians in the United States and the emerging growth of technology abroad, the Internet wields the potential to become a powerful delivery system for theological and ministerial education.

[25] Dodds, A. Administration of Distance Teaching Institutions: A Manual. Cambridge, England: International Extension College. 1983.

[26] Brey, R. "Expanding the Classroom through Technology: Meeting the Mission of Community Colleges". *Community, Technical, and Junior College Journal.* 1988.

Absent in Presence but not in Heart

Chapter Four:
High-tech or High-touch?

In spite of the great advances in technology, I think it is inarguable that students still prefer the personal interaction and innovation offered by a "hands-on" teacher. A 2002 CNN.com quick vote revealed that 33% of Americans consider innovative teachers the most important factor in achieving academic excellence; only 3% placed a priority on the latest technology. 29% considered motivated and disciplined students the most important factor[27].

Serving as a small example of this statistic, Jodie Morse, a TIME Magazine journalist, took an online course on Shakespeare's Plays from the University of California at Berkley's online extension school. She was pleasantly surprised by the course itself, primarily because of the instructor. Morse states, "The lectures were enthralling and the work demanding. The feedback from my professor, Mary Ann Koory, was voluminous, near instantaneous and often launched a spirited e-mail chain between us. I had much more contact with her than with many a teacher who presided over a packed lecture hall." Indeed, this was one case where an instructor chose innovation over idleness and elected to actively pursue a relationship with her students[28].

The greatest issues that Christian educators will face in operating in the realms of online teaching methodology are

---

[27] CNN.com QuickVote Poll, "Back to School". Internet Resource located at http://www.cnn.com/SPECIALS/2002/back.to.school/. December, 2002.
[28] Morse, Jodie. "Internet 101: The Case for Online Courses". Novemeber 3, 2000. TIME Magazine. Time, Inc.

innovation in teaching and personal interaction with the students, which ultimately leads to Accountability and Activation for ministry.

Issues of physical separation and isolation:
Autonomy & Anonymity

The challenge presented by maintaining "high touch" in "high tech" online learning is that of physical separation. Critics of distance education argue that its instructional model for learning separates teachers and students. Advocates, however, have adopted that criticism as its very definition. Distance education is intended to provide the "out of classroom" convenience to the student, identifying physical separation not as an oversight but an intention.

Isolation is sometimes preferred by the student. There are many reasons why a person may prefer the autonomy and anonymity that distance education provides. For instance, an adult student may feel uncomfortable sharing a classroom with younger students who appear to be more flippant, less concerned about learning, or even more willing to accept the instructor's personal point of view and teaching style.

With a growing number of Baby Boomers discovering online learning, this preference is becoming increasingly apparent to educators. A study published in July, 2000 by the American Association of Retired Persons revealed that 9 out of 10 adults ages 50 and over said they wanted to actively seek out learning opportunities to keep growing personally and enjoy the simple pleasure of mastering something new. Many older adults are embracing a new way of going to school: doing it online."

According to research by MediaMetrix, the online learning industry is "increasingly looking to the attractive demographic of Baby Boomers and seniors --- Now the fastest growing Internet population. That group grew 18.4% in 1999 and it's not composed of casual users: adults 50 and over actually spend 6.3 more days per month logged on the Internet than do 18-24 year olds."[29]

Mary Furlong, the founder and chairman of ThirdAge Media (an Internet company who targets an audience of people in their 40's and 50's) stated that, "The Internet can be more welcoming than a traditional classroom. At a certain point, you're not sure you belong sitting at a desk in junior college with a bunch of 22-year olds. Online, if you have gray hair, no one notices. Humor matters. Intelligence matters."

The November 3rd, 2001 edition of *TIME Magazine*, educational journalist Jodie Morse confirmed her personal desire for instructor interaction over technological wonder. Her exposé is built upon the premise that online learning can be a positive experience for graduate students balancing jobs and families, but not for undergraduate pioneers. She states, "the idea of spending four years at home looking at Windows instead of sitting in a classroom looking out windows seemed as much fun as screening prospective dates over the web instead of scoping them out in person".

Internet-based learning may best serve adults seeking graduate education or even undergraduate degree completion. For purposes of ministerial and theological education, these may be matured Christians who have served in the local church for many years, who now feel a call to ministry. Online education is best suited for this type of student, who has the ability to study on a flexible, part-time basis in their own home or church. "Furthermore, it is financially easier for students to have a full-time job at the same time as they are studying, and hence, in the absence of grants, pay their own way through school".

---

[29] Winters, Jessica. "Lifelong learners going back to class online". September 9, 2000. TIME Magazine. Time, Inc.

Absent in Presence but not in Heart

Chapter Five:
The theological accrediting bodies and online education

Accrediting associations are not necessarily the definitive authority to ensure that students are properly equipped for ministry, however many have attempted to address the issues surrounding the deficiencies of distance education in general. Section 10.3.3.3 of the Association of Theological Schools[30] accreditation standards states, "distance education programs shall seek to enhance personal and spiritual formation appropriate to the school's mission and ecclesiastical tradition and identity. Courses shall provide sufficient interaction between teachers and learners to ensure a community of learning and to promote global awareness and sensitivity to local settings."

ATS has made an attempt to force institutions to address these issues, although no clear direction is given on how to do so. Recognizing that this is a vital aspect of education, they have included the clause regarding "personal and spiritual formation" and "a community of learning". In fewer words, The Association of theological Schools has clearly made a statement regarding the importance of Activation and Accountability.

It is my understanding that ATS will not accredit solely distance education institutions. If accreditation is to be sought for distance learning curriculum, it must be supplemental to the

---

[30] The Association of Theological Schools. Pittsburgh, PA. http://www.ats.edu

fulfillment of the prescribed requirements for the residency program of the school.

The Transnational Association of Christian Colleges and Schools (TRACS)[31] refers to technology-oriented distance education programs as "innovative or experimental learning actives" which must be campus-based. In the association's Accreditation Manual, TRACS addresses the issue of Activation and Accountability in alternative learning environments:

> *"In an effort to serve new populations of students as well as the traditional student population, many of today's institutions have introduced new teacher-student relationships that differ from relationships that have been employed traditionally. In some instances these relationships differ according to the ratio of students to teachers (independent study), and the frequency, length, or mode of contact (external degree programs), while in other instances differences pertain to the mode in which the student interacts with the subject matter (experiential learning)."*

TRACS indicates that alternative student-teacher relationships exist where innovative methods of distance education are utilized. These alternative methods may vary in frequency, length and mode of contact. Frequency of interaction may vary depending on the individual needs of the student. An online learning student who is able to assimilate the subject matter and perform well in evaluation procedures may not require as much interaction as a student who desires personal interaction with the instructor. In the same way, students may differ in the length (or duration) of communication and interaction that is required. The mode of contact will vary significantly from the classroom to the online learning platform as well. The mode in which the student interacts with the

---

[31] Transnational Association of Christian Colleges and Schools. Forest, VA. http://www.tracs.org

subject matter will also vary between distance education and traditional classroom instruction.

By including this clause, TRACS has recognized that interaction and relationships between the student and the instructor, which under gird Activation and Accountability, are a necessary component of any method of educational delivery.

I do not want to labor on the regulations of the accrediting bodies, as they are actually much more detailed than the few clauses I have presented. However, it is my desire that you understand the vital role of the accrediting bodies in assuring that education programs training men and women for ministry fall under appropriate scrutiny, especially in regards to Activation and Accountability.

Absent in Presence but not in Heart

Chapter Six:
"It is not good for man to be alone."

The remainder of this book will demonstrate the theological implications of online learning, especially in training men and women for ministry, and propose possible remedies for the deficiencies that present technologies tend to create. I believe that this is the most vital concept that any online educator must grasp. I want to establish each premise on the Bible rather than mountains of educational or scientific research, as I believe it is much more of a theological matter than a technological one. I will in turn approach any additional research in light of the truths of Scripture through the perspective of a Biblical worldview. For those of us who are Christian Educators, this should undoubtedly be our focus and central concern.

The debate surrounding theological and ministerial training online has yet to have its fire kindled. This phenomenon is still in its infancy and for this reason, we have not heard it publicly discussed as much as other "hot" sociological topics that involve the Church. I believe that as it becomes more and more commonplace for pastors, teachers, and Christian leaders to pursue further education online, we will hear much more about this in the public square.

When I first began researching this concept, I determined in my own heart that I wanted to see what God has already said about it. Of course the Internet was a long ways off when the pages of Holy Scripture were written, but there are some foundational truths in God's Word from which we can develop a better understanding of what online learning means to us today.

Let's start out with a proper definition of who God is and how He has revealed Himself to us over the course of history. I believe that God is the relational God and for that very reason, He created us as relational beings. The Bible highlights many of God's attributes which express His desire for close, personal, and intimate relationships; especially with created man. We know that God Himself is triune in nature, consisting of the persons of the Father, the Son, and the Holy Spirit. The oneness of the Godhead (Hebrew: *Shema – "Hear Oh Israel, the Lord your God, the Lord is One."*) will never be fully comprehended by mortal man, but it demonstrates the depth of relationship that is to be desired and actively pursued by every Believer. This can clearly be seen in the prayer discourse of Jesus prior to His crucifixion. He stated, "I pray also for those who will believe in Me through their message, that all of them may be one, Father, just as You are in Me and I am in You. May they also be in Us so that the world may believe that You have sent me (John 17:20-21, NIV)." The intimate oneness relationship that Jesus prayed for remains inconceivable to mankind, yet it challenges the Body of Christ to pursue an intimate relationship with God and one another.

God's desire for corporeal fellowship (that is, physical, bodily fellowship) with a created order is seen in the first chapter of Genesis. It is understood that celestial, non-corporeal beings (angels and consequently demons), existed prior to the creation of this universe, with whom God had a relationship with of one form or another. God's desire to create a material universe was not merely a creative experiment, but a deliberate and purposeful engagement in a physical relationship His human race. The creation account of man demonstrates this truth. The marvelous declaration of the Creator, "Let us make man in our image, in our likeness (Genesis 1:26)", was the Divine instantiation of such a material relationship with a created universe. Adam became a living being when God formed him from the dust of the ground and breathed into his nostrils the breath of life; the very life that was given to Adam was the breath of God and the very body in which he found his being was shaped by God's own hand. Humans are therefore formed in the image of God, giving them the visible capacity to both represent the Creator and relate to Him with reason, self-consciousness, free will and imagination. This is relationship.

Out of man, God made woman (Genesis 2:21). Seeing Adam alone amidst the animals, God said, "It is not good for the man to be alone. I will make a helper suitable for him (Genesis 2:18)." God had a relationship with Adam, but he recognized that Adam needed a flesh and blood relationship --- and a flesh and blood relationship with the animals would not do. While God was Sovereign over Eden, we can only deduct from scripture that He interacted with Adam in spirit, not in flesh. He therefore formed Eve, who would be to Adam "bone of his bone, and flesh of his flesh (Genesis 2:24)".

The Word of God also describes theophanies; face-to-face, visible manifestations of God which occurred throughout Biblical history. These accounts of personal visitations of the Creator to His creation were more than literary anthropomorphisms; they were actual confrontations with God Himself, which reveal His continued to desire for a material, face-to-face relationship with humanity. Incidences such as the burning bush demonstrate the deep, intimate relationship that the fathers of the faith had with God.

Christophanies also occurred, wherein the Son of God took on a visible form at various times in the Old Testament, appearing to Adam (Genesis 17:1-4, 9-10, 15-16, 22; 3:8), Abraham (Genesis 18:1-3, 10), Jacob (Genesis 32:24-30), Moses (Exodus 3:2-6), Joshua (Joshua 5:13-15) and Daniel (Daniel 3:22-25). It should be understood, however, that the only full manifestation of God was in the form of the Son, Jesus Christ, both incarnate and preincarnate (Matthew 11:27), who was God made flesh, and who dwelt among humanity (John 1:1, 14). The incarnation of Christ, God condescending to cloak Himself in human flesh, was the final demonstration of His great love and desire to have a physical, corporeal relationship with His creation. He is forever Immanuel, God with us (Isaiah 7:14).

The tripartite formula, described by Walter Kaiser as the "hallmark of all Biblical theology"[32] also demonstrates God's desire for a material relationship with His people. The theme of "I will be your God, you will be My people, and I will dwell in the midst of you" saturates the pages of scripture. The ultimate fulfillment of this formula is seen in Revelation 21:3: "I heard a loud voice from the throne saying, 'Now the dwelling of God is with men, and He will live with them. They will be His people, and God Himself will be with them and be their God (NIV)'." Indeed, it was not good for man to be alone, and never again shall he be alone; for God will dwell with him. This will be ultimately fulfilled in the Resurrection, when we our physical bodies will be raised incorruptible in Christ and we will spend eternity with Him – theanthropus, the God-man.

Man, therefore, being made in God's image, longs for physical, face-to-face relationships as well. As we saw in the creation account, it is for this reason that God has given the gift of marriage. This desire for "real" relationship extends into the fellowship of the Body of Christ. This can most clearly be seen in the text of the New Testament Epistles. As previously stated, Paul for instance, can be seen in many ways as a distance educator. However, he too recognized the need for personal, physical, interaction with his students, not only to fulfill his own relational needs, but to ensure that proper spiritual activation and accountability were taking place.

In his letter to the Romans, Paul states, "I long to see you so that I may impart some spiritual gift to make you strong --- that is, that you and I may be mutually encouraged by each other's faith (Romans 1:11-12)." This is an incredible phenomenon which never ceases to amaze me. When you are in the company of other healthy, mature believers (especially mentors), you cannot help but be encouraged. Rev. Frank Hodges, an honorable United Methodist minister, discipled me through high school and college; some of the most critical and developmental years of my life. During my sophomore year in college, he and his family took a pastorate in a

---

[32] Kaiser, Walter. "A History of Israel", page 33.

small church in Tulare, California. That is a long way from Grove City, Pennsylvania. Although the wonders of telephone and e-mail were extraordinary, I missed being in his company; I missed our mutual encouragement. However, the vast distance that separated us and the inability to seek the presence of God together in one place could not be remedied by technology. Ironically, Rev. Hodges returned to Pennsylvania after his year of "missionary service" in California and soon after my wife and I left for our year of service in El Salvador.

I'm sure you can relate to this story in one way or another. If you've ever been away from home on a long trip, there's nothing like finally coming home and scooping up your wife in your arms. You could talk to her a dozen times throughout the day on the telephone, but until you pass through the threshold of your own home and see her face-to-face, you aren't quite fully connected. The same could be true if you've ever sent a son or daughter away to college or summer camp.

Of course, we experienced this first-hand (to a greater extent) during our year in El Salvador. We were able to e-mail photos home, talk for hours on Instant Messenger... and what was really more amazing to me was that we could talk to our family on our cell phone while we were doing a food distribution in a remote community somewhere along the Salvadoran countryside (sometimes it seemed as though our cellphone service worked better in El Salvador than it did in the United States!). Yes, technology has remarkably transformed the way we communicate, but it has not changed our need for a face to face relationship. All in all, things haven't changed that much since Paul wrote his letter to the Romans.

Paul's plea to his most notable pupil, Timothy, to "do your best to come to me quickly (1 Timothy 4:9)" also demonstrates his desire for companionship. Paul wanted to *see* Timothy, to have him laboring with him by his side. He could receive reports of what Timothy was accomplishing in other regions, and he could send

Timothy his own reports, but there was a point at which Paul simply desired to have his spiritual son by his side.

If you or your church supports missionaries, you may be able to relate to Paul's plea to Timothy in this way: think about the incredible difference it makes to actually visit the mission field to see the work that the missionary is doing. You can mail a check each month to support their work, but until you are there, on the field, seeing what they are seeing, standing beside them, you will never fully connect to their work overseas.

The Apostle John makes the most vivid and striking statements in this regard. Ending his second epistle, he says, "I have much to write to you, but I do not want to use parchment and ink. Instead, I hope to visit you and talk with you face to face, so that our joy may be complete (2 John v.12)." He reiterates this point in his third epistle, stating "I have much to write to you, but I do not want to use pen and ink. I hope to see you soon, and we will talk face to face (3 John v.13)."

Clearly these men, experienced in writing "curriculum for distance education", desired to see and talk to their pupils in a very real and physical sense. This desire is evidence of the very image of God in every man.

Let it be understood, therefore, that God, by nature, designed and desires a face-to-face relationship with humanity and by logical extension humanity also desires face-to-face relationships with one another. The challenge is not defining the necessity of such a relationship in distance education; it is defining the nature of such relationships in a digital world.

In the modern age, communication and relationships have become increasingly "virtual". This evolution began, perhaps, with the writing of letters, followed by mass media, the telegraph, the telephone, the radio, the television, and presently, the Internet. From a theological perspective, we must determine whether or not printed letters, an electronic voice, or digital video constitute the kind of relationship God intended for humanity to share with Him and with one another.

The power of the delivery system

Research has proven that Christians are at the forefront of technological usage, including the Internet. Theology has proven that God desires a physical, corporeal relationship with His people and for His people. While the Internet enhances relationships by providing easier and faster methods of communication, its methodology is not physical in nature, but virtual.

Because of the wide-reaching educational potential that the Internet proposes, Christian colleges, universities, and theological/ministerial training organizations must take steps forward in the direction of online learning. If they do, they must address the potential deficiencies of this powerful delivery system, namely, the lack of Activation and Accountability, both of which are corporeal, not virtual, functions of Christian Education ministry.

Where two or three of you *virtually* gather in His name, is He there in the midst of you?

Jesus stated, "if two of you shall agree on earth as touching anything that they shall ask it shall be done for them of my Father which is in heaven (Matthew 18:19, KJV)." The *Geneva Study Bible* suggests that the usage of the word "touching", which is normally used of the body, is here used of the mind. Although a chorus of voices in prayer joined in perfect accord, almost like a beautiful symphony, may occur within the context of a local, physical congregation, it is not necessary for God to hear and respond to prayer. Two believers may have never met and may reside on different continents, but they may agree on earth as touching something and ask it of the Father in His will, and it will be done. They may even be in agreement without knowing they are in agreement. This is the omnipresent power of the Holy Spirit who is at work in this present age... across oceans and mountains.

Jesus continued his statement above, "For where two or three are gathered together in my name, there am I in the midst of them (Matthew 18:20)", laying claim to the divine attribute of omnipresence. The presence of Christ among assemblies of believers across the globe is not His physical presence, but His spiritual presence. He is ever-present, working in the midst of every church and gathering of believers. He will not be physically present with His Bride until the resurrection, but until that day, it is Christ Himself and the Holy Spirit, working with His church (Mark 16:20) to accomplish the work of the ministry.

Because the presence Christ promised is a spiritual one, it is not unreasonable to assume that He is in the midst of those who gather in His name via telephone, video-teleconference, Internet-chat or Instant Messaging. However, it should be made clear that that which is virtual is not equivalent to that which spiritual. Anything "virtual" that mankind has constructed is dependent upon physical things. Virtual reality cannot occur without a sophisticated mass of computer chips generating the images. E-mail would not exist without the worldwide network of physical servers and data lines. Spiritual things, however, are not intrinsically dependent upon the physical universe. I believe it is important for Christian Educators to understand this truth as we continually progress into a virtual world.

The International School of Ministry (ISOM), a series of DVD courses produced by Good Shepherd Ministries International[33], has been developed on the premise that spiritual activation can and does take place through electronic replication. The courses are being translated into more than 65 major world languages and are being used to train pastors and ministers across the globe.

The tape ministry of R.C. Sproul[34], one of my most admired scholars and theologians, personally impacts me each time that I

---

[33] http://www.isom.rog
[34] http://www.ligonier.org

listen to a new message. However, as R.C. himself vehemently contends, it is not the tape, video, or even the preacher who makes the impact...it is the Holy Spirit Himself who does the work. It is also important to note that R.C. and I are not present in fellowship together; I am simply listening to a recording. I could ask R.C. hundreds of questions unceasingly, but I can't expect him to stop preaching and answer me.

I do believe that spiritual activation can take place to some extent through audio and video, but we must first remember that the work is done by the Holy Spirit, and second, that fellowship does not occur via captured lectures or sermons.

"And Lo, I am with you always"
The presence of Christ with every believer

Upon his ascension, Jesus granted his presence to his immediate disciples and to all that should succeed them in future generations. His promise was that he would be "with them always, until the end of the age (Matthew 28:20)". The Greek word used by Matthew to denote the Lord's promise of "with" was *meta*, which is a preposition literally meaning "accompaniment or occupying an intermediate position". It should be understood that Jesus did not grant his corporeal presence or accompaniment, which they would not have again until the resurrection, but his spiritual presence. That is, he would be with them, in a spiritual sense.

The promise of the presence of Christ with every believer is a spiritual one, and therefore intrinsically intended to serve spiritual (not necessarily physical) purposes. The promise of the return of Christ (John 14:28) and the resurrection of the dead (Romans 6:5) is the promise for a culminated corporeal relationship between God and His people.

The incarnation, death, and resurrection of Christ, which is the seal of promise of the resurrection of humanity (1 Corinthians 15:13), was the crowning act of God's desire for flesh and blood relationship with man and the ultimate fulfillment of man's inherent need (that is, by nature) for a flesh and blood relationship with the Creator.

"This do in remembrance of me"
Modeling the administration of the sacraments

The sacraments of the church are perhaps the best representation of functions of ministry that cannot be administered or modeled virtually. Traditional Seminary students often see their instructors serving in local congregations and therefore directly modeling ministry; an aspect of education that cannot be emulated in distance learning. Martin Luther defined a congregation as "proper administration of the sacraments". Students cannot learn to administer the sacrament of baptism over the Internet. They cannot feel the water, they cannot touch the person. Students cannot learn to administer the sacrament of Holy Communion over the Internet. They cannot break the bread or smell the wine; they cannot see the reaction of a congregate as they partake of the elements. In like manner, the proper administration of a wedding or a funeral cannot be simulated, no matter how realistic the virtualization may be.

Stimulation of the senses is not the only aspect of modeling the sacraments that should be taken into consideration. The administration of the sacraments is to be learned experientially. No where in Paul's letters does he suggest that the recipients share the Lord's Supper with him as they read; it is an act that must be shared by the people of God in a live, local context. Each sacrament is to be administered and modeled by real people to real people in a real setting.

Laying hands on the sick

The practice of laying hands on the sick and anointing them with oil (James 5:14) is another element of ministry which cannot be performed virtually. Although the sick may be prayed for beyond physical boundaries and restrictions, they may not receive the prescribed physical touch of the elder or the physical anointing of oil that scripture calls for.

"How beautiful are the feet..."

The Apostle Paul, referencing the Prophet Isaiah, exclaimed, "How beautiful are the feet of them that preach the Gospel of peace (Romans 10:15, Isaiah 52:7)". This statement gives credence to the value of a live person physically delivering Good News, wherein his or her very feet are beautiful to the hearer. While evangelism and discipleship may occur virtually online, Isaiah and Paul both placed value on a feature as simple as the feet of the one who does the work of ministry.

"I send unto you Timothy"
Spiritual Fathering by Instruction

Not only are particular functions of ministry impossible to model in a virtual environment; the very heart of Activation and Accountability are also impossible. "Spiritual Fathering and Mothering" is a concept that has become increasingly popular in recent years although its premise is age-old. Paul understood this concept fully as he wrote To Whom It May Concern: his pupils in Corinth and Thessalonica.

Paul said, "For though ye have ten thousand instructors in Christ, yet [have ye] not many fathers: for in Christ Jesus I have begotten ye through the gospel (1 Corinthians 4:15)". Paul understood that there were many παιδαγωγους ("paidagōgos" from which the English word "pedagogy" is derived), which are defined as, "boy leaders". In the Greek culture, these were typically slaves who led the boys to school. They did not instruct them, they only led them to the place of instruction.

Paul, on the other hand, stated that he was a father and that he had "begotten" his pupils. The one who leads the children to school has no intimate connection with them. He does not instruct them nor does he impart spiritual truth, nor does he model ministry. The role of fathering is reserved for the educator. It was Paul who laid the foundation for their Christian faith. Though they may have many teachers and one day a ministry of their own, it was Paul who poured into their lives during their time of intensive instruction. Because Paul had poured so intensively into them, he felt the loving affections of a father for them. Because of these affections, which were instilled and perpetuated by the Holy Spirit, Paul could admonish his pupils to be his imitators (1 Corinthians 4:16).

A potential danger in online learning is that students remain anonymous and somewhat disconnected from the instructor, thereby inhibiting the father-son relational experience. The educator must gain a true father's heart for his students; a process that cannot occur virtually.

For this reason, Paul sent Timothy to his students. He also identified him as his own son and said that he would remind the other students of himself. It was not enough for Paul to continue to write letters to them; he had to send unto them Timothy.

When Paul said that Satan had hindered him from coming again to the Thessalonians, again he sent Timothy in his stead (1 Thessalonians 2:18, 3:1-2). Paul valued Timothy and found him very useful to his ministry, but he felt it good to be alone in Athens so that someone could go to be with his students in Thessalonica. When sending Timothy to Corinth, Paul referred to him as his son, but in this instance, he referred to him as his brother, demonstrating the growing esteem for his pupil. Timothy was sent to Thessalonica to establish and comfort Paul's students.

The Thessalonians were young converts, and just planted together as a church. They suffered a considerable amount of afflictions in the early stages of their development which made Paul concerned for the longevity of their faith. Timothy was sent to make sure that the seeds that Paul had planted would grow into full fruition and they would have a firm foundation upon which they could continue to build their church. This was almost certainly done through clarification of what Paul taught and advanced instruction; functions of ministry which can only be performed by a Christian educator.

Timothy was also sent to comfort the Thessalonians, who had suffered much for their faith. Amidst suffering, seeds of doubt and fear had been sown for which the face-to-face contact of a live minister alone could bring comfort. Written letters perhaps made a minor impact and brought considerable consolation, but it did the hearts of the students well to see that Paul had sent someone as dear to him as Timothy.

Paul's personal sentiments to Timothy are also noteworthy. In his second letter to Timothy he mentions that he remembers the unfeigned faith of Lois, Timothy's grandmother, and Eunice, Timothy's mother. Paul continues by stating, "and I am persuaded that this faith is in thee also (2 Timothy 1:5)". The very personal sentiment undoubtedly impacted Timothy's development as a minister of the gospel. Paul, as a spiritual father, says to his spiritual son with full confidence, "I know your heritage, I know you, and I know that there is a call in your life; I know the faith that is in you, and I know that God has a plan for you". Immediately following Paul's encouragement, he speaks of a spiritual impartation to Timothy, wherein he physically laid hands on him and imparted a special gift to him; in a sense Paul fanned the flames of the spiritual fire which was burning inside of Timothy, preparing him to be sent out to do the work of the ministry. This type of relationship is extremely difficult in the learning environment of the Internet-based theological and ministerial training.

Likewise, online educators cannot easily model these same principles with their students. The question must be asked, "How can an Internet instructor send unto his students a Timothy?"

"Absent in presence, but not in heart"

Paul often qualified his letters by reinforcing the fact that he was absent from his students in presence but not in heart or spirit (1 Thessalonians 2:17, 1 Corinthians 5:3, Colossians 2:5). Paul's affection for his students burned fervently for them, even when he was separated from them by great physical distance. Internet educators should aspire to the same convictions for their students. Although they are separated physically, they should commit to being "present in heart". I believe that this foundational, fundamental principle will be one of the determining factors which make online learning a success or failure in the years to come.

Chapter Seven:

Avoiding the educational isolation of "autonomy and anonymity"

While physical separation is intrinsic to the definition of distance education, isolation in learning is inexcusable and dangerous at best in any instance of theological or ministerial education. Noted distance education scholar Börje Holmberg suggests that physical separation of the teacher and student "encourages greater student independence and autonomy, and the habit-forming experience of working on one's own"[35]. This may be true for the pursuit of natural science, mathematics, or engineering, but it drives a devastating blow to the heart of the ministerial calling and vocation.

Fellowship is an undeniable essential of the church and the ministerial vocation, because it naturally births accountability. Paul's belief was that personal fellowship with Christ would in turn issue fellowship among believers (1 Corinthians 10:17). To revisit, for a moment, the sacraments, Holy Communion is an indispensable mandate of the church which cannot be experienced in isolation; it must be "shared" among believers as the epitome of Christian fellowship. Paul was angry over the mockery that the believers in Corinth were making of the Lord's Supper by partaking in the sacred meal yet ignoring the needs of their brothers and sisters and creating factions and divisions (1 Corinthians 11:21). They had so focused on

---

[35] See Holmberg, B. 1979. Practice in Distance Education: A Conceptual Framework. Canadian Journal of University Continuing Education, Summer, 6 (1).

the religious act that they had denied the essential component of true fellowship, which caused Paul to speak against their gathering altogether (1 Corinthians 11:20). While physical congregation does not naturally produce Biblical fellowship, it is necessary for its healthy development.

Fellowship is a foundational principle for any ministry of the church and therefore it must be directly addressed by online Christian Educators. Paul expressed the essential need for unity in the leadership of the church by emphasizing that Peter, James, and John had extended to him "the right hand of fellowship (Galatians 2:9)". John also affirmed that fellowship with God should result in fellowship with other believers (1 John 1:3, 6-7). This type of fellowship among students and faculty produces a healthy system of accountability within the online learning environment. It is thereby reasonable to suggest that Activation and Accountability are impossible without a sufficient amount of interaction between the instructor and the student, which develops a healthy, Biblical model for fellowship.

Asynchronous communication:
"Rich content, reduced connection"

The accelerated rate of technological progress has, however, greatly bridged the gap of student-teacher separation. Issues of isolation are now being addressed by the use of audio, video and various other interactive technologies provided by the Internet. Instructors may now record classroom lectures and publish them to the Internet, allowing distance students to experience nearly the same instruction and impartation that their traditional students receive.

This "spread of teacher expertise" extends the reach of the instructor's message significantly. Where class sizes and admission was once limited by the size of lecture halls and semester units, an unlimited number of students may now experience the same curriculum and lectures (designed and delivered by the same instructor) via the Internet.

Not only do these technologies provide more personal interaction between the student and the instructor (as opposed to a textbook and study guide), they provide increased opportunity for the refinement of asynchronous communication. By recording lectures in audio or video media, instructors have an opportunity to refine and edit their own impartation and instruction. As opposed to the spontaneous, synchronous communication of a classroom environment, an instructor using multimedia-driven asynchronous communication may subject their curriculum and lectures to the scrutiny of peers and mentors[36].

The opportunity for peer collaboration establishes great potential for the delivery of instruction of even greater quality than the classroom. Teams of subject-matter experts from the same institution or even other institutions now have the opportunity to directly review and critique the instructor's performance. This method provides a model from which the quality of curriculum can continually evolve and develop.

Even if the student is experiencing a quality multimedia presentation of the curriculum, there is no assurance of direct Accountability and no opportunity for Divine Activation. While Internet technology serves as a platform for engaging the student in rich instructional activities, human interaction (in one form or another) is required for true relationship building to take place. Otherwise, the impartation and activation experience of the student is equivalent to little more than watching television or listening to a radio broadcast.

Since the advent of broadcast media, Christians have been tuning in to electronic voices and images for spiritual enrichment. In an analysis of the dilemma of broadcast media, David Gulsker states, "Few clergy or laypeople trust radio or TV ministries. These

---

[36] Guri, S. "Equality and Excellence in Higher Education – Is it Possible?". Higher Education. 1986.

ministries are thought to be manipulative, theatrical, phony and often built around ego-centered clergy. Commonly one sees signs of a "messiah complex" when watching or listening to electronic church ministers."[37]   While the peer collaboration principle for producing high quality multimedia curriculum has its advantages, it also has its deficiencies.   Students may feel as though their lectures are cued rather than compassionate.   The carefully edited, digitally re-mastered effects of television, radio, and Internet broadcasts serve as a great supplement to church life and possibly the best alternative ministry to shut-ins, but it must not be the sole source of instructional impartation.

The necessity for synchronous communication: "Information vs. Impartation"

The April 2001 edition of online *Learning* magazine reported on a survey which revealed that even the most prestigious and rigorous online degrees face limited acceptance among employers. In like manner, certain segments of "mainstream" academia also have their doubts. The September edition of online Learning highlighted the campaign against online degree programs championed by Langdon Winner, a political science professor at Rensselaer Polytechnic Institute in Troy, NY.   Dr. Winner invented the "Automatic Professor Machine", which "doles out knowledge much like an ATM at a bank". The purpose of his invention is to "stir up discussions of what online learning can and cannot accomplish[38].

Christian educators should desire to "impart" some life changing truth into their students.   This clear manifestation of Activation and Accountability cannot be achieved by means of asynchronous communication alone. In his book, *Teaching as Paul* taught, Christian education scholar Roy B. Zuck states that, "many

---

[37] Glusker, David L. "The Dilemma of Broadcast Ministry". The Christian Century, February 17, 1988.
[38] Jones, C. "The absent-bodied professor". Online Learning Magazine. September, 2001.

teachers seemingly teach as if helping students acquire facts. However, though Paul's teaching goals included gaining knowledge, they went far beyond that. [Learning means] more than a mere intellectual comprehension of information. Many of Paul's goal oriented statements and exhortations show his deep concern not only about what his readers knew, but also about what they were to be and do. These aims may be summarized in one phrase: to foster spiritual growth and maturity. This is essentially the same goal Jesus had in His ministry." The Apostle Paul and Jesus Himself recognized the need for divine impartation rather than mere delivery of information. This cannot be achieved by listening to an audio homily, watching a video or even reading carefully documented lecture notes.

Activation and Accountability, by means of impartation, occurs when the teacher demonstrates a lifestyle of ministry to the student. Zuck also noted that "teachers, like Paul, should live in such a way that they, without hesitation, can challenge their students to follow them. This is not bragging or boasting; this is simply urging others to follow Christ by their own model of being consistent and faithful in endurance, godliness, selflessness, humility, spiritual progress, and industriousness."[39] Students cannot witness firsthand the instructor being consistent, selfless, humble, or progressive by means of asynchronous communication. They see the instructor only in a single instance, in the pulpit, perhaps even in the studio... but they do not see the lifestyle that the instructor leads in his or her daily life.

The New Testament Epistles, though doctrinal in nature, are infused with personalization. Paul especially refers to people, places, and circumstances with which his pupils are intimately familiar. He also commends and admonishes them personally, often by name. Paul was so familiar with his students that he knew those who were excelling in righteousness and those who were struggling with sin. Paul's evaluation of his students was not based on a multiple choice

---

[39] Zuck, Roy B. "Teaching as Paul Taught", page 11.

test; it was based on close, transparent, revealing relationships with them.

In an online learning environment, asynchronous communication does not, within reason, provide an opportunity for instructors to develop such relationships with students. When streaming lectures are prerecorded homilies pointed in no particular direction, it is nearly impossible to fashion the virtual classroom, no matter how sophisticated, into the likeness and intensity of real life situations. Even the minor functions of the live, traditional classroom (such as the student raising his or her hand to ask a question), are non-existent in the asynchronous learning environment.

This should not discourage the use of methods of asynchronous communication for delivering information and curriculum. It simply means that some activity or interaction must augment it.

Ideally, the implementation of asynchronous communication should free the instructor to focus on the more important aspects of impartation, such as interaction and relationship building. By recording, editing and refining lectures once, the instructor has more opportunity to focus on the needs, questions, and concerns of students rather than focusing on delivering information. Dr. Stan DeKoven of Vision International University states that "the teacher is responsible for the communication"[40]. By freeing the instructor from preparing for and repeatedly teaching the subject matter, ample opportunity to initiate communication and interaction with the student should be provided.

Internet distance education provides many means for synchronous communication, the most common of which are live chat and message boards. These allow students to interact with their instructors as well as other students, both personally and publicly. While synchronous, textual communication provides an enhanced, personalized level of impartation that a generalized (recorded) lecture

---

[40] Dekoven, Stan. "Christian Education: Principles and Practice", page 19.

does not provide, it is only slightly more advanced than e-mail and it is not nearly as sophisticated as a live telephone conversation.

The March 15th, 2000 edition of *TIME Magazine* recorded the story of Internet Billionaire Michael Saylor's announcement that he would pledge $100 million dollars to the creation of an online university of, as he puts it, "Ivy League quality." His vision is to offer free education to anyone who has access to the Internet.

In sharp reaction to the announcement, TIME Digital editor Joshua Quittner argued that Saylor will face many challenges, the least of which will be financial. He believes that in the end, the biggest roadblock will be technological. Quittner stated, "Distance learning won't be ideal until major technological hurdles crumble, until we have super-fast connections to the Net that will allow people to send and receive video as easily as they e-mail each other today"[41].

Live, streaming video is still not the ultimate solution to the spiritual gap that exists between the teacher and the student. While it may greatly enhance communication even to the point of identifying personal nuances, it still does not provide the level of Accountability that is required to foster spiritual growth and maturity, because it lacks the power of physical presence, availability and community; all of which can, however, be developed in the context of the local church.

---

[41] Reaves, Jessica. "Good-bye, Quads --- It's point, click and graduate". March 15, 2000. TIME Magazine. Time, Inc.

Absent in Presence but not in Heart

Chapter Eight:
The Local Church

It is my heartfelt belief that the local church is the optimum environment in which the issues of Activation and Accountability can be directly addressed. A live and localized mentor, preferably a well-qualified pastor or lay leader, is absolutely necessary for the student to experience a complete academic and spiritual transformation.

The local church is an excellent lab environment for practical application of material learned in online lectures. Students of theology and ministry may even present the curriculum to his or her local church mentor or pastor for further interaction and review. The pastor may be able to elaborate on specific points or offer alternative perspectives, especially regarding debatable theological doctrines or issues of local church identity (that is, how the material applies to the immediate community, city, or region). Serving as a local "subject-matter expert" who knows the student personally, the pastor can offer impartation that a repetitious video or audio clip cannot.

In the local church, the student may also put into practice what was learned in theory by online instruction. It provides a supervised, hands-on setting for practical ministry. If the student is training to be a pastor, he or she may practice the administration of the sacraments. If a student is training to be a teacher, he or she may teach a class simulating a traditional student teaching experience. There is no other environment which is as accessible, flexible, or practical as the local church for experiential learning to take place and develop. Even parachurch ministries (or at least their leadership) are in one way or another accountable to a local church body.

The Community of Faith

If Internet-based theological and ministerial education programs are implemented in direct and distinct in partnership with the local church, it may prove to be a very successful method for training men and women for vocational ministry. However, if a traditional Bible College or Seminary campus does not exist, the local church is the only body which can provide adequate Activation and Accountability for distance learning students.

The local church can be formally defined as a single, geographically located, temporarily limited, visibly evident, physical manifestation of the universal Church[42]. This "community of faith" is a clearly defined subset of the Body of Christ as a whole.

The local church is a single entity, a congregation of Believers sharing a common cause, purpose, and vision. It is geographically located; not necessarily defined by the street address of a building, but the geographic region, city, or community which its people represent. The local church is temporarily limited because it is ever changing, as its people age and migrate through various stages of life. Children are born and raised, adults grow old and die. An instantaneous "snapshot" of the local church is always impermanent.

Finally, the local church is a physical manifestation of the universal Church, which is referred to as "the body" of all believers, of whom Christ is the head (Colossians 1:18). The local church is a physical manifestation of the entire body because it is comprised of corporeal human beings sharing in fellowship and community, operating in the fundamental functions of the universal Church.

The local church is an indisputable fundamental of orthodox Christianity and it serves as the best method to execute the

---

[42] Definition derived from the Study Notes of "The Open Bible – New King James Version"

components of Activation and Accountability for online learners. If a student is strategically integrated into the local church environment, he or she may study online and apply what has been learned in a very real, very corporeal environment.

Reserving practical application and "hands on" learning to the local church

The Local Church is the only place wherein practical application and the "hands on" elements of ministry can be exercised. As described above, practices of ministry such as the administration of the sacraments and the laying on of hands cannot be simulated in a virtual environment. Online educators should reserve the instruction of practical application to the local church. While theory and doctrine can be taught in an online environment, the respective application must be exercised at the local church level. This is especially true for educational institutions which cross denominational bounds. Each local church may approach orthodox doctrine in a different way, especially when administering particular sacraments.

Absent in Presence but not in Heart

Chapter Nine:
Developing strong online Christian Educators: an Apostolic Model

In his second letter to the church in Corinth, Paul provided a positive model for distance instruction which I believe can be easily translated to online learning for theology and ministry. The model which Paul and his fellow apostles established may be replicated in present day educational ministry; even if that ministry is done through the Internet.

Like the Apostle Paul, modern day Online Christian Educators will, by nature, have a great diversity of students across great physical distances. The model which Paul used to maintain integrity, academic quality, and strong activation and accountability is still applicable today in the implementation of online teaching and instruction.

The model I would like to explore is derived from Paul's account of his third visit to Corinth and of the work he would do when he arrived (2 Corinthians 13:1). He spoke of his own distance education ministry, which was administered through the writing of letters, and presented the following strategies to his own students:

1. "Now I pray to God that ye do no evil; not that we should appear approved, but that ye should do that which is honest, though we be as reprobates (v.7)". Paul and his fellow apostles prayed for their students, that they would do no evil. This was not so that

the apostles themselves would gain approval for their superior teaching skills, but only that the students would be transformed and spiritually changed. Online instructors should prepare their own hearts to be reprobates, not that they would prove the effectiveness of their own teaching skills (whether by audio, video or text) but rather with the pure motive of the spiritual transformation of the lives and ministries of their students. Especially with online asynchronous, recorded and edited lectures, instructors should guard their hearts to be sure that their only purpose is to impart truth, not to perform.

2. "For we can do nothing against the truth, but only for the truth (v.8)". Paul and the apostles, who claimed to be under the divine inspiration of the Holy Spirit, also declared that they could do nothing against the truth. Namely, they could teach no false doctrine or do anything among them that was adverse to gospel message. When an online instructor communicates synchronously with students (using message boards, e-mail, chat or the like), he or she must write or speak nothing that contradicts what they have already taught in their texts and lectures. Abrasive idioms and jesting should be avoided to remain above reproach in all things.

3. "For we are glad when we are weak and ye are strong: and this also we wish, even for your perfection (v.9)". Paul and the apostles did not need to demonstrate visibly their apostolic authority by signs and wonders alone. They did so by maintaining an attitude of humility and love. When preparing curriculum and communicating with students, online instructors should not be boastful or arrogant in writing or lectures, recollecting the many great ways in which God has used them in the past or even worse, how He "will use them in the future". Instead, they should focus on the curricula and its relevance to the lives of the students; namely, by the power of the Holy Spirit Who completes the academic work by transforming the heart and life of each student. Earlier in the letter, Paul speaks of false

apostles, who entreated on the territories of other men and made false claims in letters. Paul stated, "such as we are in word by letters when we are absent, such [will we be] also in deed when we are present (2 Corinthians 10:11)". The false apostle had "weighty and powerful letters, but his bodily presence was weak and his speech contemptible (v.10)". Paul warned his pupils against this kind of teacher who perhaps could write well in letters, but his life and ministry were for naught. When preparing curriculum online, instructors should not make great claims regarding their own anointing, ministry, or authority. Rather, it is best for them to focus on the subject matter alone. It is vital that online instructors present themselves as the exact same humble person both online and in physical presence.

4. "Therefore I write these things being absent, lest being present I should use sharpness, according to the power which the Lord hath given me to edification, and not to destruction (v.10)". Paul wrote to his students warning them to change their behavior and turn from evil before he came among them, wherein his apostolic authority would be exercised fully and would thereby bring judgment and physical punishment. Online instructors, however, should only exercise their authority for edification, bringing warning and training to their students, not judgment and discipline. I believe that such actions should be reserved for local leadership and pastoral overseers alone; they cannot be effectively enforced by an online instructor, and therefore, should be avoided altogether. For issues which require discipline or judgment, online instructors should refer the student to their local pastor (or more appropriately, refer the local pastor to the student, if possible), as many of them may never meet their students face-to-face. Instructors should focus on edification, not judgment. This is an element of divine accountability which can only occur at the local church level.

These four steps to effective online instruction can be summarized as follows:

The Online Christian Educator should:

1. Pray for transformation of the lives of the students. Beyond the absorption of the material.
2. Teach nothing false, write or say nothing offensive or regrettable via chat, message boards, instant messaging, e-mail or other live streaming communication methods.
3. Maintain humility so that deeds match teaching. Students may see only an "edited" version of the instructor's life in an online environment. If the student ever has the opportunity for live, one-on-one fellowship with the instructor, they should not be alarmed or disappointed.
4. Edify and instruct only; reserve discipline to local leadership.

These guidelines can provide a standard protocol for effective online instruction derived from traditional methods of Christian Education. They do not directly address technical issues; rather, establish a firm philosophical and theological foundation upon which Internet-based theological and ministerial education can be executed.

Praying for online students

Often, Paul and other New Testament epistle writers noted that they remembered their students in prayer. As mentioned above, a positive practice for online educators is to consistently pray for their students by name and according to any specific circumstances they are familiar with. Consistency in this regard may help the educator to develop an intimate concern for the students and their spiritual growth.

Measuring spiritual formation and maturity

Apart from academic assessment tools, the Online Christian Educator is posed with a dilemma not faced by secular educators: that of measuring spiritual formation and maturity in the life of the student. Christian Educators should be even more concerned about this dynamic because their educational ministry tends to be less "impartational" in nature than the traditional Bible College or Seminary. This is difficult to measure in online learners because of physical separation and an absence of community (both of which are not concerns for a traditional campus). Ultimately, these issues can be traced back to Activation and Accountability. The student must be activated into spiritual endeavors by the local church, whereby his or her progress can be monitored by local leadership. In like manner, close, personal, and candid accountability relationships challenge the student to strive for righteousness, spiritual formation and maturity.

The online educator does, however, have tools at hand to augment the functions of the local church. There are several methods which may aid in the effort to measure the spiritual growth in the student. Some recommendations are:

1. Implement and monitor online student journaling, now referred to as "weblogging". This exercise is not new to the distance educators, as journaling has been a process traditionally used to measure the time and energy a student puts into a correspondence course. The online journal should be accessible to the instructor, but private to the student (that is, students should not have access to one another's journals). The instructor can review daily entries into the journal and make appropriate comments via e-mail or other methods of communication.

2. Engage the student in reaction writing. Allow the student to express his or her own response to elements of the course, not from an academic or research perspective, but from a personal perspective. The student should be encouraged to write and submit short, reactionary papers that address how the content of

the course is relevant to the student's present ministry, spiritual development and relationship with Christ.

3. Encourage healthy communication with the student's local church mentor. Online surveys can serve as an excellent tool for collecting feedback from the student's mentor in the local church. The form could include general questions regarding the student's visible fruit and his or her capacity for enhanced ministry. This type of information can be gathered in the form of a Leikert Scale, which would allow for easy statistical analysis at a later date. This type of interaction not only helps maintain a positive assessment of the student, but it also helps instructors analyze and critique their own teaching effectiveness.

These measures should not be used as an attempt to substitute the vital role of the local church in the academic experience of the student. Rather, they should be used to facilitate that role and thereby better serve the student by compelling the student to pursue a deeper and more meaningful relationship with his or her local mentor.

Chapter Ten:
Online Teaching Methodology for the Christian Educator

In his letters to Timothy, Paul declares that he is "appointed a preacher and an apostle and a teacher of the nations (1 Timothy 2:7, 2 Timothy 1:11)". However, in all his power and anointing, Paul was only able to teach according to the confines of the age of his earthly ministry. Though his teaching extended possibly as far west as Spain (Romans 15:28), he was nonetheless limited by the roads and waterways of the age in which he ministered.

The church is now in a new age where global systems for communication are readily available and increasingly becoming a commodity. Christian Educators are presently faced with the great challenge of integrating this new technology without abandoning the methods of effective teaching which served Paul so well. The new systems which are capable of worldwide outreach must be utilized to their fullest within the constructs of New Testament teaching models. In other words, the challenge will not be that of content; it will be a methodological challenge. Paul did the best he could with the systems that were available to him. Today's Christian Educators must do the same.

Objectives in Online Teaching Methodology

Clear objectives establish the framework from which all methodology is derived. Paul clearly states his objective in his epistle to the Romans, "Brothers, truly my heart's desire and prayer to God for the Israelites is that they may be saved (Romans 10:1)". His objective is clear not only in this instance, but throughout his doctrinal and exhortational writings: "that they may be saved". It is upon that simple objective (for Jews and Gentiles alike) that Paul's teaching methodology was firmly established. In the same way, Jesus Himself declared his object many times as "I have come..." The well-known declaration of Christ speaks of his objective on earth, "The thief does not come except to steal and to kill and to destroy. I have come so that they might have life, and that they might have it more abundantly (John 10:10)." Clearly the objective of Christ's ministry was to "give life and give it more abundantly". From that statement, the objective of his entire ministry can be derived. His death and resurrection are products of that objective. His healing, miracle, teaching, and preaching ministry are all in line with his objective of "giving life".

It is interesting to note that Jesus first states an antithesis of his objective, that is, stating what the thief comes to do; the very things he has not come to do. Often times it is effective to state not only a clear objective for instruction, but also the things which are intended to be avoided.

In Christian Education, all objectives are intrinsically linked with some outcome of a revelation of a deeper understanding of God. Anything short of this reality is not in cooperation with the fundamental philosophy of Christian Education. Whether the student is studying New Testament Greek or Physical Science, the objective should be the same: to reveal the reality of Jesus Christ and a Biblical Worldview to the students.

When the prefabricated materials, the high-tech equipment, the multimedia presentations, and every other resource fail the instructor, the objective must be steady and unwavering. The systems are dynamic and evolving, but the objectives should remain static and unwavering.

Scripture is the single best resource for instruction. Although it does not directly prescribe modern application to Calculus or

Psychology, the Bible is the fundamental truth upon which every other truth rests. If the Bible is the primary source for all educational instruction, the objectives will not waiver. If the Word of God is in plain view and Jesus is lifted high, all teaching objectives will, by natural affinity, align themselves with Him.

Objectives in the educational realm are not quite as measurable as objectives in business. For instance, a board of directors may set an objective to reach a particular profit-margin by the end of the second quarter. A builder may set an objective to construct a building according to particular blueprints. A salesman may set an objective to reach a certain number of closed sales by the end of the month. In all these cases, there are measurable, quantitative parameters which can be assessed upon completion (or incompletion) of the project. In Christian Education, the objective to be achieved is not that of shaping pieces of material or calculating dollars and cents, but that of causing living things to grow. While visible fruit may be examined, the lives and ministries of students are not quantitatively measurable by any means on this earth, but they will be one day measured by the great Judge Himself, Jesus Christ the Lord.

I understand that "objectives" are sometimes seen as antiquated formalities required by accrediting bodies or course evaluators, but by taking the time to establish your true objectives in online education, your work will be much more effective. Whether the curriculum is being delivered via the traditional systems of the professor, classroom, and paper-based examinations or online streaming media, the objective of reaching and teaching the student must not change. If this is the case, the measurement of the success of objectives will ultimately be done by the Holy Spirit, not by any method of assessment.

Becoming a student of methodology

Because today's technology is continually changing, the modern Christian Educator must become a student of methodology. The age of chalkboards, pull-down maps, and slide projectors is long since past. Today's delivery systems require intense and diligent study.

The instructor must first become a student of his or her students. A firm understanding should be established of how the students utilize technology, online learning systems in particular; demographics maybe extremely helpful in this regard. Some students are more comfortable with reading while others prefer audio and video. The instructor should become familiar with how his or her students respond to various online teaching methods. Careful records should be kept to analyze and monitor success. Paul knew his students; he knew their cities, their culture, and their circumstances. It was because of Paul's careful study of the objects of worship of the Athenians that he was able to effectively preach the gospel to them (Acts 17:23).

The instructor must also be a student of online teaching methodology. He or she should explore the most effective uses of online learning systems and not only the technologies themselves, but also the use of the technologies. For instance, the preferable method by which audio and video lectures are synchronized with a text outlines should be carefully observed to best simulate the traditional classroom.

The instructor must know what materials should be used for online education. While nearly all materials are "virtual" in the online environment, they may be coupled with physical materials. Online materials may consist of streaming audio and video, graphics, photographs, animations, and text. Adobe Acrobat®[43] files are an excellent option for delivering textbooks and study guides online. The

---

[43] http://www.adobe.com/acrobat

instructor should become familiar with these materials and know when to use them for online instruction.

Life Integration

Whether the instructor delivers curriculum online or in person, it is vital for the student to feel as though the learning experience is integrated with his or her everyday life. Isolation tends to occur in online learning, whereby the student separates the online learning experience from everyday life experiences. Learning should not simply be considered "another technical task", such as checking e-mail. As surely as the campus environment of a traditional Bible College or Seminary becomes the central focus of the student's life during their resident experience, the online learning experience should do the same. However, as previously discussed, it cannot and should not replace absolutely necessity of the local church.

The instructor is responsible to insure that this takes place. When the student feels entirely isolated or self-guided, he or she will be less inclined to integrate the learning process into everyday life; instead, it may be viewed as nothing more than another item on the "to do" list.

"Life Integration" may be accomplished through the execution of specific methodologies in the online environment. The student should be confident that an instructor or faculty member is only a few clicks away. E-mail, message boards, and especially live chat (text or video) sessions are the best way to accomplish this goal. These methods of instruction provide personal impartation that traditional aspects of distance education often lack. Students who feel that online learning is a significant part of their life and daily experience will better respond and participate in the academic process.

Active and Passive methods of online instruction

There are generally two methods of instruction, in both the classroom and online. Passive instruction is typically marked by one-way communication from the instructor to the student. In an online learning environment, this is typically referred to as asynchronous communication (see Chapter 7). Active instruction is a two-way engagement of discussion and between the instructor and the students. This is typically referred to as synchronous communication in an online environment.

In Internet-based education, passive communication should be planned and evaluated according to its *quality* and active communication should be done according to quality as well as *quantity*. In other words, the passive communication should contain rich educational content where a few words of motivation are much more effective than two dozen repetitive ones.

Traditional methods of passive instruction

The passive methods of instruction used in the traditional classroom include typical methods of teaching such as the instructor speaking, utilization of the chalkboard, handouts, and the occasional use of audiovisual equipment, such as showing a movie or a slideshow.

Active methods of instruction in the traditional classroom include communication methods such as calling on students to answer questions, requiring students to participate by writing on the chalkboard or by working together on in-class projects and presentations.

The need for active methods of instruction

Many students learn best by doing, not watching or listening. This is typically true for distance learning students especially. Many of the passive methods of instruction in online environment are multimedia driven; they tend to be dazzling and much more visually stimulating than the traditional classroom, but they cannot replace the vital aspect of student-teacher interaction. Online instructors should always take into consideration methods by which they will integrate active methods of instruction.

Methods of passive instruction

- Textbooks are typically the most traditional method of passive instruction. They provide an organized outline of course materials in an accessible and digestible format which includes charts, photographs and self-led learning activities. In most cases, all of the information of the course is contained in the textbooks. In an online learning environment, textbooks can be stored in HTML or Adobe Acrobat Format so that they may be browsed or downloaded from the Internet. In my experience, it has been more effective to require the student to purchase the hard-copy book instead of trying to print it on their own printer or trying to read the book off of the screen.

- Lectures are usually prerecorded (although they may be broadcasted live) for the online learners. Multimedia lectures can either be derived from a live classroom situation on a traditional campus, or by an in-studio recording session. Video overlays of text, photographs, maps, charts, and b-roll video can greatly enhance the lecture in ways that are impossible to achieve in the traditional classroom.

- Lecture Notes are sometimes the most efficient way to transfer information to the student as opposed to the students taking extensive notes on a detailed issue. However, remember that note-taking is an excellent learning process, especially in distance education. The students should be provided with adequate material, but not spoon-fed.

- <u>Slide Presentations</u> are a simpler form of passive information delivery than a video lecture. There are many obvious advantages over the traditional blackboard or slideshow, but many instructors currently use Microsoft PowerPoint presentations in the classroom; these can be transferred directly to the online environment.

- <u>Hyperlinks</u> provide an advantage over normal slide shows by providing an opportunity for students to visit external websites and resources. Hyperlinks also can provide additional, more detailed information for the student who wants to explore a topic further.

- <u>Animation</u>, such as Macromedia Flash[44], can be used to demonstrate flowcharts, processes, and sequences that would otherwise be static.

Methods of active instruction

- <u>Synchronized Web Browsers</u> allow the instructor to facilitate students through the navigation of websites in real time. This method can be used to lead a class through web related activities or to explore multimedia materials.

- <u>Virtual Whiteboards</u> allow the instructor to simulate the classroom blackboard by displaying text and drawing shapes to the students in real time. The instructor may also display images and highlight information on the fly.

---

[44] http://www.macromedia.com

- <u>Audio and Video Conferencing</u> can better simulate the classroom environment, as students see the instructor presenting the material live. If properly produced, this can be an excellent simulation of traditional instruction. If accompanying video is mixed live, text can appear on the screen in place of the blackboard as the instructor is lecturing. This method also provides the opportunity for students to ask questions and interact with the instructor in ways that passive, asynchronous communication do not.

- <u>Message Boards</u> allow the students and the instructor to post messages to one another in a public "bulletin board" style environment. This method is excellent for questions and answers that would be applicable to the entire class. This method also allows students to refer back to previously addressed issues for study and review.

- <u>Text-based Chat</u> is a simple method of synchronous communication by which students may interact with the instructor live by typing text. Multiple students can participate in a discussion with the instructor and one another.

- <u>Teamwork Mechanisms</u> provide a simulated version of group work that may take place in the traditional classroom. By organizing students into groups or "teams", they may gain experience in working together with other students. Message boards and Chat may contribute to teamwork. File/document sharing should also be employed.

- <u>Online Tests & Quizzes</u> allow the student to complete assessment tools without the involvement of an instructor. Most tests and quizzes can be automatically graded online, saving the instructor time and providing the student with immediate feedback. This method works well for corrective learning opportunities.

- <u>Offline Methods</u> such as e-mail and voicemail, allow the instructor to send messages to the student that may be read at leisure. Papers and assignments may be graded and returned to the student via e-mail. This is an effective method because it is already widely used and does not require additional training or software.

Grading Online Assignments

A true educator knows the great joy of taking a red pen to a student's paper. The freedom that the pen provides to scribble notes of encouragement or correction between lines and margins is almost like its own form of art. However, in the online environment, the luxury of using the red pen is not readily available. Of course, the student's submitted documents could be printed, marked, scanned, and resubmitted to the student, but that process requires an unbearable amount of work. I still find myself printing students' assignments and marking them with a pen, then utilizing the computer to rewrite the comments; if that method is more comfortable for you and you don't mind the extra work, it can be an acceptable method for grading online assignments.

There are, however, positive, alternative methods that can be used to simulate the process of the "red pen" in grading student assignments. It will require a bit of adaptation on the part of the instructor. Following is a basic procedure which I have found to be quite successful:

1. Download the student's submitted assignment to your hard drive; preferably the file is in a rich document type such as Microsoft® Word or HTML.

2. Open the document and read it. As you read, mark mistakes by utilizing the "strikeout" command and add in the correct phrase or word in parentheses. For instance, "the Gospel was given to the ~~Gentlies~~ (Gentiles)". Preferably, make all corrections in red.

3. If you would like to comment on a particular part of the student's work, I suggest inserting your comments directly in the flow of the paragraph. Begin your comments with an indicator, such as "Instructor's Comments:". Your comments should also be in red.

4. The best advice that can be given is to simply take advantage of the flexibility of a Word Processor. You have all the space you need to work with, which actually gives you, in some way, more flexibility to the traditional pen.

5. Resubmit or resend the assignment to the student, with your changes integrated. *Note: Most recent version of Microsoft® Office support correction tracking features. I suggest not using this feature at this point as it can be a bit clumsy for the student.*

Successful Methodology

Successful online instruction requires a fundamental understanding of online methodology. There are many methods by which instruction may be conducted in the online environment. The instructor should understand the technological opportunities and restrictions of his or her teaching ministry, establish firm objectives, become a student of methodology, and strive to integrate the learning experience into the student's everyday life. If methodology is properly implemented, online instruction can be a successful and meaningful experience for the distance learning student which is far superior to the traditional methods of correspondence coursework.

Absent in Presence but not in Heart

Chapter Eleven:
Using Chat and Messaging for Communication

"Chat" has become a buzzword of the present generation as well as a daunting enigma falling to the criticism of parents and educations. Nevertheless, text-based chat has remained an effective form of synchronous communication.

Finding its primitive beginnings in the age of Morse code across telegraph lines, developing into bulletin board systems and now the Internet, chat is by no means in its infancy. With decades of opportunity for evolution, development, and transformation, the fundamental elements of present day chat has remained virtually unchanged. It remains a viable and quite reasonable text-based synchronous communication method.

Well-managed and focused chat sessions can provide a powerful online learning experience and synchronous student-student and student-teacher interaction. However, because chat is difficult to monitor and manage, many instructors hesitate to utilize it in online learning environments. The more traditional, asynchronous methods of e-mail and message boards tend to be more widely accepted.

Internet chat often has a negative reputation because of its potential to become chaotic as students and instructors are communicating simultaneously. The standard flow of classroom conversation tends to become clumsy and difficult.

A carefully planned chat session can greatly enhance the online learning experience. The spontaneity of chat can be a great contrast to the static content of an asynchronous course. Through chat, the voice that students are listening to on streaming audio lectures comes to life and responds to their personal questions and comments. The thought of a live instructor in "real time" may radically affect the student's passion for learning in an online environment.

Types of Chat Sessions

There are many types of chat sessions that the online educator may implement in order to encourage community among students. Many students who may have been uncomfortable in a classroom setting may feel more comfortable communicating with text-based chat because social inhibitions have given way to pure communication. Below are some examples of creative ways in which Chat can be utilized:

Virtual Group Projects

Online instructors may establish teams of students who work together on a class project. The planning sessions and "brainstorming" for the project may take place in the course chat room or a private room, where the subset of students can discuss plans, ideas, and aspirations for the assignment. Progress can also be discussed and critiqued in a collaborative chat environment.

Distance learning students will gain much more experience with team work, especially in a modern business world, by working together and communicating with a team online.

Exam Preparation

One of the deficiencies of Distance Education that many students struggle with is the inability to discuss class material with other students and study for examinations. Chat allows students to collaborate and ask one another targeted questions about uncertainties and areas of particular difficulty. This type of communication among students should be strongly encouraged, as opposed to e-mailing questions to the instructor only.

Prayer Requests and Fellowship

Students may enjoy the element of fellowship that chat provides. They may use chat to share prayer requests and pray for one another in real time. Chat provides an opportunity for students to "gather" in the name of Christ that they may experience His presence together as classmates (Matthew 18:20). One of my Christian Ministries professors at Grove City College, Dr. Randy Stringer, made a strong impression on me when he took the time to ask for personal prayer requests at the beginning of each class and carefully offer each of them up to the Lord. I believe the same kind of care can be applied to the online learning environment.

Oral Quizzes

Instructors may also elect to conduct oral quizzes with their online students by scheduling a time, taking attendance and asking questions. This type of assessment is most effective in a one on one chat session as opposed to a group setting because targeting specific students with questions in chat may become awkward. Instructors may also utilize the live environment of Internet chat to follow up with students whom they may suspect have plagiarized or not entirely read or comprehended the required texts for the course. This allows the instructor to ask very direct and targeted questions in rapid sequence. The student will not have time to "look up" the answer in a textbook or online.

Chat-based Virtual Office Hours

Instructors may choose to be available for live question and answer sessions for scheduled "virtual office hours", wherein the students may sign into the chat room and know that their instructor is there waiting, ready to answer questions. Instructors may also elect to invite guest speakers during their office hours and encourage students to attend. Students may be able to ask course relevant questions to someone with a different perspective than the assigned instructor.

Teaching Language

Chat provides a tremendous method for teaching foreign and biblical language classes via distance education. Ministerial and Theological educators may quiz Greek or Hebrew vocabulary and grammar in a chat session. A multicultural studies or mission instructor may evaluate the progress of students learning a second language. While it does not account for dimensions of voice inflection or pronunciation, the precision of text is, in many ways, superior to traditional classroom methods. Special fonts can also be used, as necessary.

Planning a Chat Session

Students, as well as instructors, will need adequate time to become proficient and comfortable with chat as an effective method of instruction and communication. Chat should not be as central to the course as the traditional classroom is; rather, it should be used as a supplement to the course requirements, providing opportunities for creative learning activities and in-depth discussions on focused topics.

Students' grades should not be based on chat sessions because not everyone works comfortably in this environment and not everyone will be able to attend scheduled sessions. Some universities make it clear that chat is not a required component of online courses.

In order to make chat sessions successful, they must be carefully planned and strategically prepared by the instructor. The best way to approach this is for the instructor to prepare an outline for the session ahead of time. The session should have clearly defined start and end times. If the duration of the session is not communicated to the students, chat sessions may become lengthy and unmanageable. The instructor should assume the responsibility of focusing the chat on the prescribed topics.

Some instructors pre-type questions ahead of time and paste them into the chat window. This saves much "typing time" and permits the instructor to spend more time to evaluate the responses of the students. If the instructor intends to take record of student responses, he or she should also have a spreadsheet prepared ahead of time, which provides a simple format for logging student responsiveness and apprehension of course content. I strongly recommend both of these methods.

The instructor should also communicate chat etiquette ahead of time. Students should be aware of what is acceptable and what is not acceptable in the chat environment.

An Educational Philosophy for Chat Sessions

The technology that the Internet provides radically changes the traditional philosophy of distance educating by adding valuable, synchronous communication. When properly implemented, chat sessions can greatly enhance the effectiveness of any online instructor. The personal dimension of chat can augment the static content of any course and provide an opportunity for students to interact with one another.

Chapter Twelve:
Principles for Practice

I would like to summarize everything I have presented so far in some very practical principles that you can utilize in your online educational ministry. Please remember, above all else, that the Internet is indeed a powerful delivery system for theological and ministerial education, but its inherent deficiencies, namely, the lack of divine Activation and Accountability must be forthrightly addressed. This can be accomplished by utilizing the extensive power of the Internet as a supplement to the ordained functions of the local church for ministerial training. If a student is unable to attend a traditional Bible College or Seminary, he or she may effectively utilize the worldwide accessibility and rich multimedia environment of Internet education, within the proper boundaries of aggressive local church involvement and accountability.

Principles and Practice

1. Christians, as a general population, are at the forefront of technological advancement and Internet usage. They are therefore prepared to utilize online learning for theological study and ministerial training.
2. As Third World nations develop technologically, the Internet will serve as a powerful resource to deliver theological curriculum. Many of these nations are experiencing phenomenal church growth, which further necessitates the urgency to deliver training on a large scale, across vast geographical regions.

3. If the Internet is to serve as a vehicle for such an awesome educational endeavor, its deficiencies, for purposes of ministerial and theological training, must be forthrightly addressed. The principal deficiencies may be defined as follows:
   a. Isolation – Students training for vocational ministry should not be separated from the Body of Christ; they should be surrounded by mentors, peers, and students of their own. Consistent, candid communication is vital to educational development.
   b. Autonomy – Students training for vocational ministry should not be independent learners. The success of their future ministry is dependent upon their ability to interact with and love God's people. A solitary passion for God does not produce abiding fruit.
   c. Anonymity – Students training for vocational ministry should be personally known by their instructors. They should be engaged not only in an academic relationship with the facilitator of a course, but they should be in covenant relationship with a spiritual father or mother.
4. These deficiencies of online learning may therefore produce a failure to address two fundamental components of Christian education (especially for those specifically training to enter full-time ministry): Divine Activation and Accountability.
5. Asynchronous communication methods only partly address this issue. Prerecorded lectures (whether video or audio) should not serve as a substitute for an interactive instructor; they should free the instructor for more interaction with the students.
6. Synchronous communication via the Internet is a positive method for interaction between the student and instructor and between students themselves. Methods such as e-mail, message boards, chat, and live streaming audio and video all contribute to virtual methods of interaction; however, they do not address the necessity for corporeal interaction.

7. Mankind has been created with an inherent desire for corporeal relationships. In more ways than not, the work of the ministry and functions of the clergy on earth must be administered through corporeal means; primarily because the Church on earth consists of corporeal beings.

8. Christian Educators may effectively reach, teach, and minister to their students when working within prescribed guidelines which reserve certain functions to the local church. It is possible for an educator to be separated by hundreds or thousands of miles from his students (as Paul was separated from his students) and still properly instruct and train students for theological and ministerial purposes; this most effectively occurs when working in direct partnership with local church leadership.

9. A student must therefore be accountable to the pastoral staff (and/or prescribed mentor) of his or her local church. He or she must also be properly activated by the local church, who imparts life changing love into the student's ministry.

As technology continues to rapidly evolve, Christian Educators will be faced with many more challenges and discover many more solutions in the great task of delivering curriculum and training to a worldwide audience. The Internet is undoubtedly the most powerful and wide-reaching tool the Church has ever seen, and it must be fully understood and properly utilized for academic purposes within the Body of Christ.

The Internet and all of the promises it wields are a new wineskin, a "digital wineskin", which Christians must use to deliver the discipleship that is desperately needed by students worldwide. It is technology which is cost effective, accessible, and continually developing. Perhaps the most encouraging fact is that Christians are not intimidated by its vastness or corruption and are using it readily.

I believe Christians will continue to learn to utilize the Internet for educational purposes in the realms of Theology and Ministry. However, as Internet technology presently stands, the best method for Christian Educators to follow is that of Paul and the other New Testament writers; communicating in word with physically distant students, but never eliminating the necessity of flesh and blood relationships and Divine Activation and Accountability; that is, always keeping the student strategically tied to the local church. By working within this Biblical model, Christian Educators can be certain that, Lord willing, the greatest harvest is yet to come.

Appendix A:
Issues of educational unity

The new edition of J. Gordon Melton's "Encyclopedia of American Religions" describes 2,630 U.S. and Canadian religious groups, categorized into 26 "families of faith". Rising above all Spiritualist, Psychic, and New Age cults, Pentecostals were found to be the most divided religious sect, containing at least 325 distinct groups[45]. Unity is desperately needed within the Protestant-Pentecostal movement; perhaps this will take place in the academic arena through the platform of the Internet.

On August 29, 2001, The Council for Christian Colleges and Universities (CCCU) Student Academic Programs Commission released a memorandum to its members announcing the availability of three online courses developed by Christian University GloablNet, an undisputed leader in online delivery of Christian curriculum. The courses included, "Foundations of the Old Testament", "Foundations of the New Testament", and "Foundations of Christianity: Early Church to the Great Shism". Following discussions regarding content, pedagogy, and delivery of the courses with CUGN staff and faculty who have used aspects of the course materials in their own

---

[45] Associated Press, The Youngstown Vindicator, "Families of Faith", February 08, 2003.

teaching, the CCCU recommended that member institutions consider utilizing the courses[46].

The memorandum stated, "In recommending this join project, we recognize the significance of attempting to encourage the use of Bible and Church History introductory courses in a collaborative manner across the many theological traditions represented in the CCCU. We have recommended to CUGN and [Colorado Christian University] that these courses be taught in ways that affirm orthodox Christian faith and that recognize and respect differing opinions of interpretive issues." The memorandum ended on a positive note: "As often true, all of us may be able to accomplish more working together than any of us could do on our own."

While this type of unification by means of sharing educational resources is occurring in some instances, it is far from universal. Many Universities and theological training organizations share curriculum and resources with local churches, but typically with their respective denomination only.

The Internet has the potential to disrupt the stagnation of unity within educational circles, providing a powerful platform upon which partnerships and curriculum sharing can take place. Many Christian Educators prefer to construct their own "branded" educational material to serve their own networks of schools and students, but the Internet now provides the opportunity for great advancements toward cooperation to occur in the realm of theological and ministerial training.

---

[46] CCCU. "Report and Recommendation on Three Online Courses". Council for Christian Colleges & Universities. August 29, 2001. Washington, DC. Found Online at http://204.176.38.91/doclib/20011102_SAPC_Report.pdf

Appendix B:

Using Internet technologies to effectively accommodate various learning styles

Educational Theories have attempted to address the differing learning styles that exist among students when approaching teaching methodology. The Internet provides an excellent platform to provide students with a rich environment upon which they can excel and develop their own individual learning styles. This type of instructional designed for online instruction is referred to as "adaptive learning".

Students who are audio learners may prefer to listen to a streaming audio lecture, which they can fast-forward and rewind at their own pace. This is certainly a triumph over the traditional classroom.

In a similar fashion, visual learners can have instant access to view and review video clips, photographs, maps and charts at leisure.

Kinesthetic learners may enjoy the engaging online activities of journaling, message boards, and online project and assignment completion. These students will also gain their greatest experience from "hands on" practical application in the local church.

Rod Sims, a professor of instructional design at Deakin University in Melbourne, Australia cautions, that "we need to learn more about how people interact with technology before we can understand how to make adaptive learning work"[47]. This is perfectly understandable from a theological perspective. Christian educators must gain a clear understanding of what "virtual" communication and instruction can and cannot accomplish *spiritually* before educational theories are addressed. Such is the case with adaptive learning. The Christian educator should focus on addressing the spiritual issues of Activation and Accountability prior to adapting and refining online curriculum to meet various learning styles.

If implemented properly, adaptive learning in an online environment can meet the needs of a variety of students and provide for a rich educational experience, but time and energy should first be focused on the spiritual needs of the student.

---

[47] Shank, Pati. "Out with the old". Online Learning Magazine. Found online at: http://www.onlinelearningmag.com/onlinelearning/magazine/article_display.jsp?vnu_content_id=1224573

Appendix C:
The dark side of the Internet

The Internet has caused many believers to cower in fear of its rampant exploitation by the "dominion of darkness (Colossians 1:13)". The very same *Christianity Today* study that yielded high percentages of positive Internet usage among pastors also unfortunately revealed that a high number of pastors are involved to some extent with Internet pornography. More than half admit that it is their strongest online temptation. About two in five (43%) have fallen to temptation at least once. More than a 36% admitted to having visited a pornographic web site in the last year.

While the Internet will undoubtedly be a powerful delivery system for Christian Education in the years to come, instructors and students alike should be aware of the Internet's open door to pornography and worldly lusts. Many safeguards exist today to shield Christians from all of the temptations of the Internet. Apart from the well-known filters such as "NetNanny", many online accountability groups exist to help monitor Internet usage. Upon enrolling in an online accountability program, the URL of every website visited is sent back to the service, making the browser's history unalterable and viewable by the peer accountability partners. This is an excellent way to keep students, teachers, and pastors accountable while making good use of the power of the Internet for educational and ministerial purposes.

Absent in Presence but not in Heart

Bibliography

1. *ACCESS* (Extending Christian Education). http://www.accessweb.org

2. Associated Press, *The Youngstown Vindicator*, "Families of Faith", February 08, 2003.

3. Association of Theological Schools (ATS), "Accreditation Standards Documentation, Section 10". April, 2003. Pittsburgh, PA.

4. Baker, Jason D. "Baker's Guide to Christian Distance Education". Baker Book House, November 2001.

5. Barker, B.O., Frisbie, A.G., and Patrick, K.R. "Broadening the Definition of Distance Education in Light of the New Telecommunications Technologies". *The American Journal of Distance Education*. 1989.

6. Barna Research Group (1), "More Americans are seeking Net-based Faith Experiences"; May 21, 2001. Internet Resource located at http://www.barna.org.

7. Barna Research Group (2), "More Christians Embrace Technology"; June 12, 2000. Internet Resource located at http://www.barna.org.

8. Brey, R. "Expanding the Classroom through Technology: Meeting the Mission of Community Colleges". *Community,*

Technical, and Junior College Journal. 1988.

9. Bridis, Ted. "Cyberspace is driving America's Economy," Pittsburgh Post Gazette, Vol 71, no. 259, 4/16/98.

10. CCCU. "Report and Recommendation on Three Online Courses". Council for Christian Colleges & Universities. August 29, 2001. Washington, DC.

11. Clark, T.A. "Distance Education: Its Effectiveness in Terms of Academic Achievement". Unpublished Masters Thesis, Southern Illinois University at Carbondale. 1987.

12. CNN.com QuickVote Poll, "Back to School". Internet Resource located at http://www.cnn.com/SPECIALS/2002/back.to.school/. December, 2002.

13. Conner, David. "Distance Education: Why Not?" http://www.accessweb.org/updates/whynot.pdf

14. Cooler, D. "Evaluating Distance Education Programs". *Canadian Journal of University Continuing Education.* Summer, 1979.

15. Cooler, D. "Using Integrated Information Technologies for Out-of-Classroom Learning". *Technologies for Learning.* San Francisco, 1987.

16. Crooks, S. "Distance Education in a Developing World". *European Journal of Education.* 1985.

17. DeKoven, S. Christian Education: Principles and Practice. Vision Publishing, 1996.

18. Demy, Timothy J. "Technology and Theology: Reality an Hope for the Third Millennium", in Issues 2000: Evangelical Faith and Cultural Trends in the New Millennium, edited by

Mal Couch (Grand Rapids: Kregal, 1999).

19. Dodds, A. <u>Administration of Distance Teaching Institutions: A Manual</u>. Cambridge, England: International Extension College. 1983.

20. Gates, William., "Introduction publication to Microsoft .NET services". 2001 Promotional Publication. Microsoft Corporation.

21. Glusker, David L. "The Dilemma of Broadcast Ministry". *The Christian Century*, February 17, 1988.

22. Guri, S. "Equality and Excellence in Higher Education – Is it Possible?". *Higher Education*. 1986.

23. Hales, R.L. "Meeting the Need for Off-Campus Professional Education". *TechTrends*, January-February, 1987.

24. Holmberg, B. 1979. <u>Practice in Distance Education: A Conceptual Framework</u>. Canadian, Journal of University Continuing Education, Summer, 6 (1).

25. <u>Holman Bible Dictionary</u>. 1991, Holman Bible Publishers.

26. Jenkins, Philip. <u>The Next Christendom: The Coming of Global Christianity</u>. Pennsylvania State University. Oxford Press.

27. Jones, C. "The absent-bodied professor". *Online Learning Magazine*. September, 2001.

28. LaRue (1), John C. Jr., "The Internet: A blessing or curse for pastors?". March/April 2001. <u>Christianity Today</u>. Christianity Today International.

29. LaRue (2), John C. Jr., "Special Report: Churches and Computers". July/August 1999. <u>Christianity Today</u>.

Christianity Today Intl.

30. Morse, Jodie. "Internet 101: The Case for Online Courses". Novemeber 3, 2000. TIME Magazine. Time, Inc.

31. Pew Internet & American Life Project, "CyberFaith: How Americans Pursue Religion Online", December 23, 2001; Internet Resource located at http://www.pewinternet.org.

32. PCUSA – "Global Education and International Leadership Development". Online resource located at: http://www.pcusa.org/globaled/kinsler.htm

33. Rao, Madanmohan, "Governance of the Internet", CPSR Newsletter, Fall, 1998, 16(4).

34. Reaves, Jessica. "Good-bye, Quads --- It's point, click and graduate". March 15, 2000. TIME Magazine. Time, Inc.

35. Servatie, Alain et all: "European Community Cooperation with Countries in Transitation and Developing Countries in Telecommunications and Information Society", in Health, Information Society and Developing Countries, Editor Marcelo C. Sosa-Tudicissa et all, IOS Press 1995. Online Resource found at http://www.uni-muenster.de/EthnologieHeute/eh1/afe.htm.

36. Shank, Pati. "Out with the old". Online Learning Magazine. Found online at: http://www.onlinelearningmag.com/onlinelearning/magazine/article_display.jsp?vnu_content_id=1224573

37. Stanton-Rich, Michael. "What will it take? Some questions about technology and the Church". Internet Resource. http://www.theooze.com/articles.

38. Stone, Martin. "Study Shows 300 Mil Worldwide Web Users" Newsbytes, excerpted in: ACM TechNews, Volume 2, Issue 34: Friday, March 24, 2000.

39. Talcott, Alexander. "Education Online?". The Dartmouth Review.

40. <u>The Holy Bible</u>. King James and New King James Versions. 1997, Thomas Nelson Publishers, Inc. Nashville, TN.

41. Transnational Association of Christian Colleges and Schools (TRACS), "Accreditation Manual". Revision December, 2001. Forest, VA.

42. Van Deventer, Jack. "The Academic Transition". *Eschaton Magazine*. December, 2000.

43. Vlach, Michael J. *"How people of faith are using the Internet"*. Online resource located at: http://www.pastors.com/article.asp?ArtID=2071 or http://www.theologicalstudies.org/internet.html

44. Wilson, W. <u>The Internet Church</u>. Gospel Light Publishers.

45. Winters, Jessica. "Lifelong learners going back to class online". September 9, 2000. *TIME Magazine*. Time, Inc.

Absent in Presence but not in Heart

Scripture References

1. Genesis 1:26
2. Genesis 17:1-4
3. Genesis 17:15-16,22
4. Genesis 17:9-10
5. Genesis 2:18
6. Genesis 2:21
7. Genesis 2:24
8. Genesis 3:8
9. Genesis 32:24-30
10. Exodus 3:2-6
11. Joshua 5:13-15
12. Proverbs 21:17
13. Ecclesiastes 4:9-12
14. Isaiah 52:7
15. Isaiah 7:14
16. Daniel 3:22-25
17. Matthew 11:27
18. Matthew 18:19
19. Matthew 18:20
20. Matthew 28:19
21. Matthew 5:14-18
22. Matthew 9:17
23. Mark 16:20
24. John 1:1, 14
25. John 10:10
26. John 14:28
27. John 17:20-21
28. Acts 17:23
29. Romans 1:11-12
30. Romans 10:1
31. Romans 10:15
32. Romans 14:18
33. Romans 15:28
34. Romans 15:6
35. Romans 6:5
36. 1 Corinthians 10:17
37. 1 Corinthians 11:20-21
38. 1 Corinthians 15:13
39. 1 Corinthians 4:15-16
40. 1 Corinthians 5:3
41. 2 Corinthians 10:10-11
42. 2 Corinthians 13:1
43. 2 Corinthians 4:15
44. 2 Corinthians 5:9
45. Galatians 1:10
46. Galatians 2:9
47. Galatians 4:19
48. Ephesians 1:12,14
49. Ephesians 5:10
50. Colossians 1:10
51. Colossians 1:13
52. Colossians 1:18
53. Colossians 2:5
54. 1 Thessalonians 2:17
55. 1 Thessalonians 2:18
56. 1 Thessalonians 3:1-2

57. 1 Thessalonians 4:1
58. 2 Thessalonians 1:12
59. 1 Timothy 2:7
60. 1 Timothy 4:9
61. 2 Timothy 1:11
62. 2 Timothy 1:5
63. James 5:14
64. 1 John 1:3,6-7

www.ingramcontent.com/pod-product-compliance
Lightning Source LLC
LaVergne TN
LVHW011404080426
835511LV00005B/409